Supermarine Spitfire

Supermarine
Spitfire

Chaz Bowyer

PRENTICE-HALL, INC.
ENGLEWOOD CLIFFS, NJ
A Bison Book

Library of Congress Cataloging in Publication Data

Bowyer, Chaz.
    Supermarine Spitfire.

    (A Reward book)
    "A Bison Book."
    Bibliography: p.
    1. Spitfire (Fighter planes)   2. World War, 1939–
1945—Aerial operations.   I. Title.
UG1242.F5B68   1983   940.54'4941   83-4496
ISBN 0-13-875807-7 (pbk.)

10 9 8 7 6 5 4 3 2 1

ISBN 0-13-875807-7 {PBK.}

This book is available at a special discount when ordered in
bulk quantities. Contact Prentice-Hall, Inc., General
Publishing Division, Special Sales, Englewood Cliffs, N.J. 07632.

Prentice-Hall International, Inc., *London*
Prentice-Hall of Australia Pty. Limited, *Sydney*
Prentice-Hall Canada Inc., *Toronto*
Prentice-Hall of India Private Limited, *New Delhi*
Prentice Hall of Japan, Inc., *Tokyo*
Prentice-Hall of Southeast Asia Pte. Ltd., *Singapore*
Whitehall Books Limited, *Wellington, New Zealand*
Editora Prentice-Hall do Brasil Ltda., *Rio de Janeiro*

Page 1: AR501, a Mark Vc, painted in No 310 (Czech) Squadron's
wartime markings, now regularly flown at displays.
Page 2-3: PM631, a Mark XIX, in full flying condition.
Page 4-5: AB910, a Mark V, painted to represent a 92 Squadron
aircraft.

CONTENTS

INTRODUCTION

Although the history of man-controlled flight stretches over a mere 77 years – the equivalent of one man's lifetime – within those years the airplane has drastically changed the very natures of both war and peace for the human race. Aircraft have been used with telling effect in two world wars and scores of lesser conflicts, and certain individual aircraft designs have achieved lasting fame on an international scale. Of these perhaps the most famous was the superb Supermarine Spitfire – a fighter which became a legend in its own era and which continues to evoke acclaim among all generations. It was also probably the most aesthetically-pleasing airplane ever to be built, adding sheer beauty of line to a fighting reputation second to none.

The Spitfire was unique in at least one respect, since it was the only Allied fighter to enter full production prior to 1939 which continued to be produced until after 1945. In all more than 22,000 Spitfires (including Seafires) were built, in more than forty major variants and a host of subvariants of differing degrees of importance. Such variants differed either greatly or minutely, depending on the intended operational role or contemporary need, but for the sake of clarity these can be divided into three main categories:

      a) Merlin-engined
      b) Griffon-engined
      c) Naval counterparts

To list and detail every possible variant would be tedious to the reader, and indeed unnecessary in this condensed account. A plethora of published literature about the technical history of the Spitfire is readily available to the 'nuts-and-bolts' archivist (see Bibliography). Accordingly, in this book the phases of Spitfire development and use are mainly restricted to those of greatest significance in terms of the contemporary scene. Equally, where performance figures are quoted specifically these should not be taken as necessarily concrete for all Spitfires of that given Mark or type.

Finally, this book is intended not only as a brief record of the Spitfires' birth, life and achievements but also as a tribute to the men and women who designed, built, maintained, flew and especially to those who died in Spitfires.

Chaz Bowyer, Norwich, 1980

Left: Spitfire (MH434) in typical Fighter Command markings for the mid-1944 era. It is a Mark IX, the serial is spurious.
Right: A Mark XIV (top) and Mark V formate.

Above: Supermarine S6b, S1595, the aircraft which ultimately captured the Schneider Trophy for Britain on 13 September 1931 at Calshot, Hants.

Above Left: Reginald Joseph Mitchell, CBE, AMICE, FRAeS, chief designer for Supermarine Aviation and 'father' of the Spitfire.

Below: First of the many; the prototype Spitfire K5054 in the guise first seen by the public.

GENESIS

On 5 March 1936 a dozen men gathered informally on the tarmac bordering the large grass airfield at Eastleigh Airport; among them were several leading aeronautical engineers of the Supermarine aviation works at Woolston, near Southampton, including Alan Clifton, head of the technical office, Reginald J Mitchell, the firm's chief designer, George Pickering and a slightly-built, dark, young ex-RAF pilot, Jeffrey Quill. From the interior of the nearby ramshackle shed which served as Supermarine's 'flight hangar' was wheeled a remarkably small single-seat monoplane, as yet unpainted and untitled but bearing the neat serial number K5054. The aircraft was prepared for flight and the bulky figure of ex-Flying Officer Joseph Summers – 'Mutt' as he was universally known – soon settled into the diminutive cockpit. Taxying out across the undulating grass, Summers turned the aircraft's nose into the wind, revved to full boost, then smoothly got airborne westward across the field. Once in the air Summers was so delighted with the new aircraft that he gave the tiny clutch of spectators below a brief display of precision turns and immaculate banking before bringing it gently back to earth. On climbing out of the cockpit Summers summed up his reactions very succinctly, 'I don't want anything touched' – the first Spitfire had passed its initial air test with flying colors.

The birth of the Spitfire fighter was no flash of inspired genius by an individual but the culmination of a gradual, reasoned progression of ideas from a combination of many people. Its chief designer was Reginald Joseph Mitchell, a brilliant young engineer who was born in Stoke-on-Trent in 1895. He joined Supermarine in 1916 and within four years had been appointed as the works' chief engineer. During the next ten years Mitchell was ultimately responsible for creat-

ing and fashioning a long line of successful maritime aircraft, ending with the series of sleek 'S' floatplanes which eventually captured the coveted Schneider Trophy for permanent possession by Britain, and established a new World Speed Record in excess of 400mph – both of these achievements taking place in 1931. Thus Mitchell and his team of designers and engineers had accumulated a vast amount of knowledge of the aerodynamic problems associated with high-speed flying when they turned to the possibilities of producing a fast fighter design for the Royal Air Force. In practice, however, this transition from floatplane to landplane design was not as simple as was first thought. The Schneider Trophy winners had been essentially 'one-off' flying freaks, incapable of military application or development. Each had been simply a 'one-shot' flying engine, designed to last relatively few flying hours and custom-built for the unique conditions pertaining to ultra-fast speed racing in the sky.

Structurally, the Schneider seaplanes were impossible to adapt for the necessary inclusion of armament, fuel and the sustained performance ranges expected from a Service machine in everyday squadron use, although the myriad lessons learned about streamlining, shaping and constructing high-speed aircraft were available to incorporate in any fresh design. The initial impetus to the eventual Spitfire design came in the autumn of 1931 when the Air Ministry issued Specification F.7/30, seeking a replacement for the standard Bristol Bulldog fighter then equipping RAF front-line squadrons. This specification, dated 1 October 1931, called for a day and night fighter design capable of carrying full oxygen, wireless and radio equipment, four machine guns and stowage for 2000 rounds of ammunition. Minimum performance figures stipu-

Above: **Supermarine Type 224, designed by R J Mitchell – his first landplane – for Air Ministry Specification F.7/30. It first flew in February 1934.**

lated included a level speed of at least 195mph at 15,000ft, a service ceiling of not less than 28,000ft and a rate of climb permitting the aircraft to reach 15,000ft in no more than eight and a half minutes. Although no particular powerplant was mentioned in the document, the most powerful in-line engine then available to British manufacturers was the Rolls-Royce Goshawk of 660hp. Other points mentioned as desirable were good maneuverability, ease of routine maintenance and a capability for rapid production in quantity.

A significant omission from the specification was whether such a fighter should be of biplane or monoplane configuration. Hence, of the eventual eight contenders for Air Ministry approval to Specification. F.7/30, five were biplanes and only three monoplanes. The latter included Supermarine's entry for the competition, the Supermarine Type 224, a low-winged monoplane with a fixed, 'trousered' undercarriage and slightly cranked wing, which represented Mitchell's first venture into designing a landplane. After the Type 224 design was accepted in August 1932, an Air Ministry contract for the construction of one prototype was awarded and the aircraft, serialled K2890, first flew in February 1934. Despite its compliance with most of the original specification's parameters, the Type 224 performed less impressively than many of its rivals and the competition winner was a biplane, the Gloster SS37, which eventually saw RAF service as the Gloster Gladiator. Mitchell himself was by no means satisfied with the Type 224, particularly its Goshawk engine, and set to work on a cleaner derivative design before the crooked-winged monoplane first appeared. His last project, designated initially as the Type 300, commenced as a private venture, that is, not government sponsored. However within a month of submitting the proposed design to the Air Ministry Supermarine was granted £10,000 for the construction of a single aircraft to Mitchell's 'improved F.7/30 design.'

Shortly afterward Supermarine contracted with Rolls-Royce to fit this latest project with a new engine, the PV-12, later named Merlin. It was the major turning point in the development of the Spitfire. This 'marriage' of Merlin and airframe gained immediate Air Ministry interest and led to the issue of a 'new' Specification, F.37/34, dated 3 January 1935 which in effect updated the former specification to the potential of the PV-12-engined Type 300. A major requirement still retained from Specification F.7/30 however, was for armament comprising just four .303in caliber machine guns; although in early 1935 the latest Air Ministry fighter requirement, as specified in Specification F.10/35, was to state that at least six, '. . . preferably eight,' machine guns were necessary. This farsighted condition can be traced to early 1933 when

Squadron Leader Ralph Sorley (later, Air Marshal Sir Ralph, KCB, OBE, DSC, DFC) of the Operational Requirements Department at Air Ministry calculated that eight machine guns would be essential in fighters if a truly lethal strike was to be made on any enemy bomber in the two seconds' engagement envisaged as the maximum time available to any fighter pilot of the future. Sorley's proposals did not gain immediate approval from all quarters of higher authority. The contemporary Air Officer Commanding-in-Chief of the Air Defence of Great Britain (forerunner of Fighter Command), Air Chief Marshal Sir Robert Brooke-Popham, expressed his personal view that, '. . . eight guns was going a bit too far. I should have been content with four.' He also added that these should necessarily be fitted close to the cockpit, and further expressed opposition to the idea of enclosed cockpits. Fortunately such views were in a minority and Sorley's proposals found favor with his superiors, being ultimately ratified by Air Marshal Hugh Dowding, then Air Member for Research and Development from 1930–36, who was later to command Fighter Command during the crucial Battle of Britain in 1940.

The Spitfire was now ready for the next stage of development and late in 1935 the new fighter – already named Spitfire, despite Mitchell's comment on first hearing the name, 'Sort of bloody silly name they *would* choose!' – began to take shape in Supermarine's Woolston factory on the shores of the Solent. By then a new elliptical-shaped, thinner wing had replaced the former derivative's straight-edged planform; the cooling of the new Merlin engine had been solved by the fitting of a new ducted radiator; and the wings now housed a battery of eight .303in Browning machine guns. Finally, on 5 March 1936, 'Mutt' Summers took up the prototype K5054 on its initial testing flight. Sent soon after to Martlesham Heath for Service trials, the prototype Spitfire created a very favorable impression, displaying a maximum speed of 349mph at 16,800ft, a climb rate to 20,000ft in eight minutes and twenty seconds and a service ceiling of 35,400ft. The trials report then commented, '. . . simple and easy to fly and has no vices.' The Spitfire's obvious potential led the Air Ministry to issue a production order for 310 machines even before this report was officially completed; while Specification F.16/36 then set out the Service needs and consequent minor modifications to be incorporated in all production Spitfires of this first batch for RAF use. This contract, signed on 3 July 1936, was part of the recently introduced RAF expansion Scheme 'F' which called for at least 300 Spitfires (and 500 Hawker Hurricanes) to be in RAF service by March 1939.

As the Spitfire – Mitchell's greatest triumph in aeronautical design – was about to enter full mass production, its designer died. For several years Mitchell had been a victim of cancer so that in March 1937 his condition was pronounced incurable and he was given just three months to live. On 11 June 1937 Reginald Mitchell finally succumbed, at the early age of 42. His position as Chief Designer for Supermarine was taken over by Joseph Smith, former chief draftsman in Mitchell's team, who was to oversee all subsequent Spitfire production development through the following eight years. Little more than two weeks after Mitchell's tragic death his brainchild made its first public appearance when, on Saturday 27 June, Spitfire K5054, resplendent now in an overall pale blue livery, flashed above the upturned faces of a multitude of spectators at that year's annual RAF display at Hendon airfield. As it astonished the public below with its fluid maneuverability and beauty, few onlookers were aware that this 'Father of the Few' (as it came to be dubbed) had cost the tax-paying public a trifling £15,776 – a financial investment which was to pay dividends beyond price in Britain's future security.

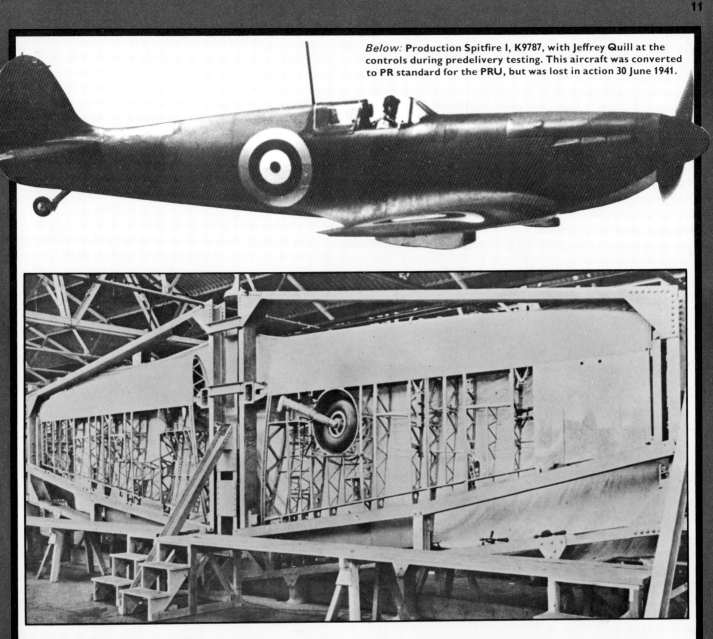

Below: Production Spitfire I, K9787, with Jeffrey Quill at the controls during predelivery testing. This aircraft was converted to PR standard for the PRU, but was lost in action 30 June 1941.

Above: The famous Spitfire wing in a production jig, revealing the internal rib structure, undercarriage housing, and 'empty' sections awaiting installation of machine guns.

Below: The prototype Spitfire, K5054, with (in background) a Supermarine Walrus (K5780), Vickers Wellesley prototype (K7556) and the Vickers Wellington prototype (K4049).

INTO SERVICE

Mass production of the Spitfire presented a number of technical and organizational problems to Supermarine. Their Woolston works simply had insufficient capacity to undertake the whole initial order and therefore considerable subcontracting was undertaken almost from the start of manufacture. By agreement, the Nuffield Organisation acted on an agency basis and a new factory was opened at Castle Bromwich for main production, while hundreds of small agents undertook parts' manufacture and assembly during subsequent years. Basically, Spitfire construction did not lend itself easily to the mass production methods then in use in Britain because it required relatively extensive (and expensive) special tooling and jigging. These problems apart, a change in overall administration and organization occurred in October 1938, when Vickers (Aviation) Ltd and Supermarine Aviation Works (Vickers) Ltd came under the single aegis of Vickers–Armstrong Ltd, the latest merger in a series of industrial reorganizations which can be traced back to 1928 when the original Supermarine firm had been acquired by Vickers.

This merger came several months after the first production Spitfire left the factory. Spitfire K9787 was flight tested in May 1938, to be followed shortly after by K9788; both machines were then retained by the manufacturers for further extensive testing. Thus the first Spitfire to enter RAF service was

K9789, the third production model, which arrived at RAF Duxford on 4 August 1938 on issue to 19 Squadron – the first RAF squadron selected to re-equip with Spitfires. Spitfire production at this period only permitted further issues on roughly a weekly basis, though by 13 October – on which date Spitfire K9802 became the first example to arrive at Duxford's other squadron, No 66 – production had begun to speed up noticeably. Soon both Nos 19 and 66 Squadrons had been brought up to full strength of sixteen Spitfires each, while three more units – 41, 74 and 54 Squadrons respectively – were all equipped with Spitfires by March 1939. In the following two months these were joined by 65 Squadron and two Auxiliary Air Force (AAF) squadrons, Nos 602 and 611. The haste in rearming the RAF was partly a natural result of the various expansion schemes finally inaugurated in the mid-1930s, but almost equally due to the operational strength (or lack of it) in September 1938, the month of the 'Munich Crisis.' At that time only three of the RAF's fighter squadrons were flying monoplanes – the Hurricanes of Nos 111, 3 and 56 Squadrons – while the remaining 27 squadrons were still equipped with obsolescent biplane fighter designs.

The change from open-cockpit, fabric-skinned biplanes to the enclosed canopy, metal-covered Spitfire gave a tremendous boost to the morale of most RAF fighter pilots of the period. Adolph 'Sailor' Malan, later to become probably the

Below: Spitfire Mark I, P9450, of the first production batch P9305-P9584, ordered on 29 April 1939 and delivered to the RAF commencing 20 January 1940. This aircraft served with 64 Squadron and was lost in action on 5 December 1940.

greatest RAF fighter leader of World War II, was a Flying Officer serving with 74 ('Tiger') Squadron in 1938, when he and a fellow 'Tiger' pilot collected his squadron's first Spitfires in February 1939. 'It was like changing over from Noah's Ark to the *Queen Mary*' said Malan later. 'The Spitfire had style and was obviously a killer. We knew that from the moment when we first fired our eight guns on a ground target. Moreover she was a perfect lady. She had no vices. She was beautifully positive. You could dive till your eyes were popping out of your head, but the wings would still be there – till your inside melted, and she would still answer to a touch.' Malan's eulogy was to be echoed by thousands of subsequent Spitfire 'drivers,' each of whom came to fully appreciate the docility of control, yet lethal potential of the Spitfire. Nevertheless, the abrupt change from Gauntlets, Gladiators and Fury fighters was not entirely free from accidents. In particular several pilots with years of experience in flying fixed-undercarriage aircraft completely forgot that the Spitfire's slender undercarriage was retractable, resulting in a small crop of belly-landings and shattered propellers.

Above: Squadron Leader Henry Cozens (nearest) in K9794 leading an echelon of 19 Squadron's Spitfire Is on 31 October 1938. Tail squadron numbers were painted on mainly for this occasion – a press facility – but were removed soon afterward.

Experimental tests and modifications were already in hand by mid-1939 to improve both the Spitfire's performance and armament. In June one machine, L1007, was fitted with 20mm Hispano cannons and fire tested the following month at Orford; though faults in the shell feed produced disappointing results. In July that year trials were undertaken at Martlesham Heath with a Spitfire (K9795) fitted with a controllable pitch airscrew which resulted in a maximum speed of 368mph being reached at an altitude of 18,400ft, while further provision for a three-blade, all-metal airscrew – originally envisaged in Specification F.16/36 – became standard in all Spitfires after the 78th production machine. Other refinements included a bulged canopy cover to accommodate the heads of tall pilots, and many minor internal improvements to pilot efficiency and personal comfort. As the final months of the uneasy peace slipped away in Europe, full production of Spitfires was stepped up. By September 1939 a total of 2160 Spitfires (excluding the prototype) had been ordered by the Air Ministry; 1000 of

these from the new Castle Bromwich works, and the remainder from Vickers Armstrong (Supermarine) and the preceding firm of Supermarine Aviation (Vickers).

Within the RAF, re-equipment of first-line squadrons remained relatively modest as the sands of peace filtered out, and on 3 September 1939, when Britain formally declared war against Germany, a total of only 400 Spitfires were in service – twelve squadrons, including five AAF units, plus reserves awaiting issue, less than a third of Fighter Command's overall strength in squadrons at the operational 'sharp end.' These compared with seventeen Hurricane units, with the remainder equipped with obsolete biplanes or hastily converted Blenheim I bombers. During the first few days of war the Spitfire pilots waited in readiness for the expected massive onslaught by the German Luftwaffe, but waited in vain. In a period of high tension and excitement, errors occurred, as on 6 September when a false radar sighting initiated a fighter alert in southern England. During this 'Battle of Barking

Left: **Well-publicized view of a 65 Squadron formation of Spitfire Is taken in August 1939. Pilots (from nearest K9906) were Roland Tuck, Brian Kingcome, George Proudman, Gordon Olive, 'Nick' Nicholas and Sergeant MacPherson.**
Top: **Spitfire Ias of 611 ('County of West Lancashire') Squadron, AAF at Digby in February 1940.**

though occasional victories were claimed; on 20 November when a 'Vic' of three 74 Squadron Spitfires, based temporarily at Rochford, caught a Heinkel III reconnaissance aircraft near Southend and shot it into the sea – the first Spitfire victory for an England-based unit. Andrew Farquhar of 603 Squadron AAF, who had claimed his first victory on 16 October 1939, added two more Heinkels to his 'bag' in February 1940. He was personally awarded a Distinguished Flying Cross by HM King George VI at 603s base airfield on 26 February – believed to be the first DFC awarded to a Spitfire pilot.

At a time when all RAF fighters were expected to undertake both day and night interception roles, many attempts were made to employ the Spitfire by night – a role for which it was neither designed nor suitable. The result was that in the first four months of the war no less than sixty accidents, some fatal, occurred among the Spitfire squadrons. With its narrow-track undercarriage and high, lengthy engine cowling, a Spitfire was difficult to handle at takeoff and, especially, landing in the black of night. Moreover the glare of the engine's exhausts merely blinded a pilot when airborne, thus nullifying any chance of a pilot seeing raiders – there being no radar fitted to any fighters at this stage of the war. Nevertheless, night flying continued to be undertaken by most Spitfire squadrons during early 1940, resulting in a further crop of accidents and injuries.

For the first eight months of war all Spitfire squadrons were based in Britain, a deliberate policy of Hugh Dowding, Air Officer Commanding-in-Chief, Fighter Command, who permitted only other types of fighters (Hurricanes, Gladiators *et al*) to accompany the Army's expeditionary forces based in France. Thus until May 1940 such engagements with the Luftwaffe as had been made by Spitfires had been exclusively against German bombers or reconnaissance aircraft. The Spitfire had yet to match its qualities against its German counterpart, the Messerschmitt Bf 109E fighter. Though it was not until June 1940 that an intact, captured Bf 109E-3 was evaluated against a Spitfire in performance and combat maneuverability, it had already been acknowledged in RAF circles that the Hurricane was the more suitable type for service in the 'field' conditions of service in France with the British Expeditionary Force. With its wide-track undercarriage and generally robust construction, the Hurricane could cope well with unprepared landing grounds and near-primitive maintenance conditions, whereas the Spitfire required rather more sophisticated conditions in support. In any case, by late 1939 there were substantially more Hurricanes available for service across the Channel than there were Spitfires, and Hugh Dowding was already looking ahead to the possible consequences for Britain of German occupation of French territory, which would automatically increase the dangers to Britain of an airborne assault. With the Spitfire's acknowledged edge in speed and high-altitude performance over the more rugged Hurricane, Dowding was determined to reserve as many Spitfires as possible in Britain for the metropolitan defense force.

Those first eight months of wary, probing, isolated combat, now universally labelled the 'Phony War' period, gave the British-based Spitfire squadrons little opportunity to test themselves operationally. On 10 May 1940 the Phony War ended abruptly and savagely, as German air and ground forces rolled forward into France and the Low Countries in a devastatingly rapid advance – the true *blitzkrieg* (lightning war) had begun. From that date all fighter units in southern Britain were put in a state of immediate readiness to commence offensive patrols across the Channel whenever required. The moment of truth had finally come for the Spitfire.

Creek' (as the fiasco was later titled) two Spitfires from 74 Squadron shot down two Hurricanes of 56 Squadron, killing one of the latter's pilots – the first Spitfire 'victories' of the war.

The first true blooding for the Spitfire came on 16 October 1939. In the early afternoon a section of 602 Squadron AAF, accompanied by three Spitfires from 603 Squadron AAF, both units being based at Drem in Scotland, set out to intercept an incoming raid of nine Junkers 88 bombers from 1/KG.30 heading for the naval anchorage at the Firth of Forth. In the subsequent brief clash two Ju 88s were shot down, one by each squadron, into the sea. On 28 October the same two AAF squadrons were in action again when a Heinkel III bomber, riddled with bullet holes, was forced down on the Lammermuir hills by Flying Officer Archie McKellar of 602 Squadron AAF – the first Luftwaffe aircraft to descend on British soil during the war. In the ensuing winter months there were relatively few encounters with German aircraft over Britain,

16

Above: **Flight Lieutenant John Bisdee, DFC of 609 Squadron, AAF** begins his taxy-out in Spitfire Ia, PR-O, at Drem in early 1940. Airmen to steady the wingtips were necessary due to the Spitfire's narrow, stalky undercarriage on the uneven grass surface.
Below: **Spitfire Ia of 602 Squadron, AAF** during the Battle of Britain – probably at Westhampnett airfield (now Goodwood) – with trolley accumulator plugged into the engine, ready for start-up.

SOME OF THE FEW

The now-legendary Battle of Britain is officially defined in RAF archives as extending from 0001 hours on 10 July 1940 to 2359 hours on 31 October 1940. These are the dates which encompass the period of operational flying considered to be the qualifying period for the official award of the 'Battle of Britain Star' – the gilt rose emblem sewn centrally upon the ribbon of the 1939–42 (later amended to become 1939–45) Star medal. All aircrew members who flew at least one fully operational sortie during this period qualified for the little 'rosette' emblem. While no one would question the qualifications of those crews who were thus acknowledged as participating in the Battle of Britain, it is a highly debatable question whether these men should be the *only* recipients of the special emblem. The significance of the two months preceding the qualifying period was far greater than most official accounts indicate. From 10 May 1940 – when the German blitzkrieg in Europe commenced – the British-based elements of Fighter Command were steadily drained of pilots and aircraft to bolster the French resistance to the German advance. While no Spitfire unit was dispatched to French soil, the burden of responsibility for defense of Britain became heavier on the shoulders of the dwindling fighter force based in England as more and more Hurricane, Gladiator and other units crossed the Channel to join the fighting.

The UK-based Spitfire squadrons in May and June 1940 were necessarily concentrated around the southeastern counties, under the aegis of No 11 Group, Fighter Command, commanded by Air Vice-Marshal Keith Park, a New Zealander with long experience in fighter operations. Within ten days of the start of the German assault the British Expeditionary Force (BEF) in France was being forced to retreat toward the Channel coast, and Park was urgently requested to provide additional air cover over the retreating Allied armies. By then Park had at his immediate disposal some 200 fighters spread thinly among sixteen squadrons in the south. His only reserves comprised the remaining fighter units stationed further north tasked with the defense of the industrial Midlands and northern England. On 26 May the order came to inaugurate Operation Dynamo, the plan to evacuate the BEF centered on the coastal resort of Dunkirk. Aerial protection for this evacuation was placed squarely upon Park's shoulders, with a vociferous Admiralty virtually demanding 'continuous air cover' over the beaches while its shipping lifted the BEF from French coastal zones, an almost impossible task with Park's slender resources.

Knowing only too well the limitations of his available fighter force, Park decided to dispatch single squadrons on a rotation patrol basis over the French coastal areas to a depth of approximately ten miles inland. In this fashion he was at least in a position to attempt to thwart any large Luftwaffe bombing forays heading for the evacuation zones. During those crucial days of late May, Park's Spitfire squadrons had their first real experience of combat with the Luftwaffe in strength. Many Spitfire pilots who had impatiently marked time for the past eight months of war fired their wing guns 'in anger' for the very first time. Among the latter were such men as 'Sailor' Malan, Roland Tuck and Douglas Bader, all of whom registered their first combat victories during the final days of May and early June 1940 while patrolling above the evacuation beaches around Dunkirk. It was also the period in which the Spitfire first clashed in any numbers with its German equivalent, the Messerschmitt Bf 109E. Despite the flurry of wartime propaganda produced about the relative merits of these two principal designs, the 1940 Spitfire Mark I was in most ways roughly equalled by the Bf 109E variant, though most pilots agree that the Spitfire was the better in terms of maneuverability and ease of handling. However, all such comparisons are invidious since there are a host of variables such as individual tactics, contemporary role and – perhaps above all – the quality and fighting spirit of the man at the controls to be taken into account.

By 18 June the last exhausted RAF personnel in France returned to England – the battle for France was over. From 10 May until 4 June (the official end of Dynamo) the RAF alone had expended a total of 432 Hurricanes and Spitfires (mainly Hurricanes). In return it had claimed a high proportion of the 1300 or so German aircraft lost in action during the same period. Across the narrow Channel a victorious Luftwaffe settled into new French bases and began its initial refurbishing and replenishing preparatory to the expected continuation of the war against Britain. The weeks immediately following the BEF's retreat from Dunkirk have often been regarded in the past as some form of lull in the aerial war, thus offering Hugh Dowding a welcome opportunity to rebuild his defenses prior to the Battle of Britain. In fact the aerial activity around England's southern shores continued daily throughout June and early July, mainly in the form of reconnaissance sorties over England, and deliberate bombing assaults on the many merchant shipping convoys bringing vital materials to Britain via the English Channel. Such supplies were desperately needed by Britain and Keith Park was again charged with provision of an air escort/cover for these convoys. His solution in this context was to send out sections of four to six Spitfires or Hurricanes on patrol, whenever the coastal radar posts detected any buildup of German aircraft heading toward the Channel. Combat, though usually involving relatively small numbers, was frequent during such convoy-cover sorties. During the first nine days of July alone, Fighter Command lost 28 aircraft but claimed at least 56 Luftwaffe victims. Yet none of the 23 RAF pilots killed or wounded in these combats were entitled to a Battle of Britain Star.

The Battle of Britain itself has been well recorded in a host of books, journals and features, and this is not the place for a detailed description. However the part played in the Battle by Spitfires is highly relevant. On 7 July 1940 – three days prior to the 'official' start of the Battle – Fighter Command could muster a total of 52 squadrons throughout Britain, nineteen of which were equipped with Spitfires, 25 with Hurricanes and the other eight with miscellaneous semi-obsolescent aircraft types. (See Appendix 3 for actual dispositions.) The most vital Groups, Nos 11 and 12, which were to bear the brunt of the overall Battle in the months ahead, comprised forty squadrons, 21 of them equipped with Hurricanes and just thirteen with Spitfires. Though this ratio was to alter almost daily at the peak of the August and September fighting, thanks to Dowding's policy of rotating tired and fresh units between northern England and the battle areas, it reflects the constant quantitative preponderance of Hurricane squadrons which fought through that fateful summer. Moreover, historical research emphasizes that more Hurricanes were actually employed during the Battle of Britain than all other fighter types combined, and accounted for nearly eighty percent of the known victories claimed. Patently, such figures merely confirm that Hurricanes were available in larger numbers than Spitfires. The Hurricane had entered service and mass production for the RAF more than a year before the Spitfire.

In theory the differences between the Hurricane and the Spitfire in terms of top speeds, climb rates et al were sufficient for Dowding and Park to allocate each to a separate tactical role. The slower Hurricane could be used to tackle the unwieldy German bomber formations at the lower levels, while the faster Spitfire would take care of the high-flying Messerschmitt fighter cover formations. In actual practice there was seldom time to set up such a fighting partnership and either type of fighter simply tackled the first enemy formations they encountered after being 'scrambled' to intercept. The bulk of Spitfires flown in the summer of 1940 were Mark Is, powered by 1030hp Rolls-Royce Merlin engines, fitted with three-blade propellers, capable of a top speed of slightly more than 350mph at 19,000ft. Basic armament remained as eight wing-housed .303 Browning machine guns for the vast majority of Spitfires in the Battle, but at least one heavier-armed version saw brief combat then. This was the Mark Ib, armed with two 20mm Hispano cannons, and 19 Squadron was re-equipped with Mark Ibs at the end of June, flew 'service trials,' then took their cannon-armed fighters into action in August. By the end of the same month, however, the squadron had become frustrated by constant feed stoppages and jams in the ammunition supply, and were reallotted a batch of eight-gun Mark Is to continue combat flying. Another Spitfire variant to see action in mid-1940 was a number of Mark IIs which began reaching first-line squadrons by July, though in no significant numbers. Full re-equipment of any unit with IIbs was not feasible until after the Battle of Britain. The Mark II was essentially a Mark I, built exclusively at the Castle Bromwich works, powered by a 1175hp Merlin 12 engine. As such it incorporated during manufacture most of the modifications and other improvements found necessary and/or desirable to standard Mark I airframes, including 73lb of armor plate for protection of the pilot and nose fuel tanks.

Although basically produced as Mark Is or IIs, a variety of minor subvariants of each Mark were also made in 1940–41. Several were logical attempts to improve endurance and range of what had been originally conceived as a home defense interceptor fighter. Various overload tanks for additional gasolene or oil were attached under wings or fuselage, while others introduced special racks and chutes for smoke or marker bombs, flares and dinghy packs for use with the burgeoning air-sea rescue services then becoming vital. It was the beginning of a long process of stretching the original Spitfire airframe design to its limits over the following five years, thereby reflecting the huge potential for development inherent in Mitchell's brainchild. All war weapons must be successively modified or improved in efficiency and performance under the hammer pressure of events, yet the Spitfire's versatility in this context was virtually unmatched by any other comparable design in its era.

Often the differences between designated Marks or subvariants of Spitfire were not immediately apparent to an outside observer. Indeed, even marked changes in structural outline were no criterion of identification of particular Marks. Nevertheless, by 1945 the possible distinctive versions and

sub-versions of Spitfire actually constructed or modified, or simply improved, ran into hundreds. Even these do not necessarily include numberless Spitfires which were individually 'hacked about' on front-line units by squadron ground crews at the behest of necessity or, on occasion, pilots – few of which were blessed with the approval of higher authority.

Notwithstanding the sterling efforts of the Supermarine team to improve the basic Spitfire during 1940, the Battle of Britain remained a triumph for the Spitfire Mark I version. Its chief adversary was the Messerschmitt Bf 109E, and in May 1940 a Bf 109E-3, originally captured by the French in November 1939, was sent to the RAF, Farnborough for evaluation and comparative trials with a Spitfire Mark I. Flown in turn by Roland Tuck and the ex-Schneider Trophy pilot George Stainforth, the two fighters were put through a series of realistic fighting maneuvers in a mock dogfight, and compared on particular facets of their respective performance limits. The resulting report in July 1940 credited the Spitfire with greater superiority at altitudes of some 4–5000ft and as being generally faster, more maneuverable and easier to handle than its counterpart. Such results gave a rather optimistic outlook because the fighting trials had been conducted along tactical lines then in use by the RAF, whereas the Luftwaffe's fighting tactics were very different, using the Bf 109E in ways in which its actual advantages over the Spitfire could be exploited fully.

In parallel, the Luftwaffe also tested a Spitfire I against a Bf 109E and one of the test pilots was the leading German fighter ace of the time, Hauptmann Werner Mölders, who said of the Spitfire, '. . . It handles well, is light on the controls, faultless in the turns, and has a performance approaching that of the Me 109. As a fighting aircraft however it is miserable. . . .' Mölders' comments applied to a captured Mark I, fitted with the old two-speed propeller and thereby decidedly inferior in climbing rate to the Messerschmitt. Yet again the German trials had taken place at altitudes and in tactical maneuvers currently favored by the Luftwaffe. Thus each nation tended to produce opinions and results favorable to their own fighter design, albeit unwittingly. In actual combat during the Battle of Britain, however, the chief arena of fighting proved to be at an altitude range somewhere between the two fighters' best height for ultimate superiority. In these conditions the Spitfire's outstanding maneuverability and roughly comparable performance made it equal to, if not slightly superior to, the Bf 109E. On an individual basis, however, the performance of *any* fighter, in *any* situation depends in the final analysis on the quality of the man flying it. In this context both the Spitfire I and Bf 109E were served splendidly by pilots whose courage, training and will to fight and conquer cannot be decried.

Above left: Mark Ia of 19 Squadron returns to Duxford after battle, September 1940. Note the 'blown' gun ports, indicating that the guns have been fired.
Below: 'A' Flight of 92 Squadron touching down at Manston airfield. Nearest, QJ-D (X4272), was one of the rare Mark Ibs used operationally, armed with twin 20mm cannons.

Above: Spitfire IIas of 65 Squadron at Kirton-in-Lindsey, Lincs on 18 July 1941, about to take off for an offensive sweep.
Above Right: Mark Vb, BM590 of 121 'Eagle' Squadron; the second of three American-manned Spitfire squadrons formed within the RAF, 1940-42, before being transferred to the USAAF on 29 September 1942.
Right: Spitfire P7973, a Mark Va conversion from a Mark II airframe, which saw service with Nos 222, 452 & 313 Squadrons before going to Australia on 23 February 1945 as a museum exhibit. At one period it was flown by the Australian ace Keith 'Bluey' Truscott, DFC.
Below: Spitfire IIs getting airborne from Northolt in the summer of 1941, while in the background another squadron forms up.

DAY OFFENSIVE

As the daylight conflict over southeastern England petered out with the onset of winter in 1940–41, the Luftwaffe switched its main operational efforts toward a night-bombing 'blitz' of Britain's cities and centers of civilian population. For Fighter Command it meant the beginning of a lengthy and frustrating, though ultimately successful, counterdefense in the night skies, a nocturnal struggle in which Spitfires played little part. Instead, on 20 December 1940, two Spitfires from 66 Squadron based at Biggin Hill slipped across the Channel and calmy strafed Le Touquet airfield, meeting no opposition. It was the modest initial sortie of an ever-increasing day offensive by Fighter Command over enemy-occupied Europe during the following years – 'leaning forward' against the common enemy. Having demonstrably won the defensive battle over Britain, the Command's policy was now to be almost entirely toward the offensive, seeking out the Luftwaffe and inviting combat on terms favorable (ostensibly) to the RAF. On 10 January 1941 a Blenheim bomber squadron was escorted by no less than six fighter squadrons during a raid against targets near Calais – the first Circus operation – but Luftwaffe opposition was small. Further sweeps were flown over enemy-occupied territory, attempting to bring up the *jagdgeschwadern*, but the depleted German fighter arm in France – many units had been transferred to the new Russian campaign in the east – seldom took the bait unless it already had the advantages of surprise and height before any engagement.

For the opening rounds of the day offensive Fighter Command relied mainly on the Spitfire II, though the need for constant improvement in fighter performances had been implemented by both air forces since 1940 in the unceasing striving for air superiority. The Mark II Spitfire was on a par in most respects with the Messerschmitt Bf 109E, the chief antagonist during 1940, but a more powerfully engined variant, the Mark V, began reaching RAF squadrons from March 1941. This latest Mark offered three main forms of armament. The Va carried eight .303 Browning machine guns, the Vb a mixture of two 20mm Hispano cannons and four .303 Brownings, while the Vc could be fitted with either 'battery' or a four-20mm cannon wing armament, plus carriage of a 500lb bomb under the fuselage. The Mark V's introduction slightly preceded the Luftwaffe's latest version of the Bf 109, the F-variant, but remained Fighter Command's chief weapon throughout 1941 for its increasing daylight assaults. The two latest fighters first met over Britain on 11 May 1941, when a Mark V Spitfire of 91 Squadron from Hawkinge shot down a Bf 109F attempting a sneak low-level bombing raid. In the event Mark V Spitfires were built in greater quantity than any other variant, a total of 6479, representing almost thirty percent of all Spitfires ever constructed.

Throughout 1941 and the early months of 1942 the air war over Europe became dominated by the fighter offensive, with the Spitfire Mark V as the RAF's prime tool for destruction. It was a period in which a host of RAF fighter pilots established themselves as fighting leaders of lasting fame; men like 'Sailor' Malan, 'Al' Deere, 'Paddy' Finucane, 'Widge' Gleed, 'Jamie' Rankin, 'Dutch' Hugo, 'Kiwi' Crawford-Compton and a hundred others. It was also a year which saw the RAF lose some of its near-legendary names. 'Tin-legs' Bader and 'Lucky' Tuck were shot down and made prisoner, while other stalwarts of the 1939–40 battles made their ultimate, fatal sorties – Eric Lock, Mungo-Park, Willie McKnight and others of equal prowess. The skies over France became a backcloth for vast armadas of Spitfires – on occasion as many as 500 on a single sweep – challenging the Luftwaffe to combat, smothering airfields and installations with bombs and attacking communications and transport of every description. The cost to the RAF was high numbers of casualties, as relatively inexperienced junior pilots met some of the Luftwaffe's finest fighting aces, but the overall offensive seldom faltered. The 'muscles' of Fighter Command were extended by a growing number of non-British pilots – Poles, Czechs, Belgians, Free French, Dutch, Norwegians, Canadians, South Africans, New Zealanders, Australians, and other foreigners. By the autumn of 1941 three Spitfire squadrons, 71, 121 and 133, had been formed as all-American units – the 'Eagle' Squadrons – and these joined the offensive until 29 September 1942, when all three were officially transferred to the American Eighth Air Force and re-equipped with American fighters. Other Spitfires to bear US markings were those issued to the first American fighter squadrons' personnel who arrived in England from mid-1942; a temporary measure until suitable American-designed fighters became available.

If Fighter Command felt any complacency about the Spitfire Vs ability to deal with the latest Messerschmitt Bf 109F it was soon to be abruptly shattered in the overall context of fighter design supremacy. On 17 August 1941 Vicky Ortmans, a Belgian pilot with 609 Squadron, returned from a combat with about twenty German fighters and was adamant in his report that one of his opponents had been '. . . a Messerschmitt with a radial engine.' RAF Intelligence refused to believe him, but clear evidence that such a machine existed became available after a Circus operation on 13 October. It was the newly-operational Focke-Wulf Fw 190. Its superiority over all contemporary RAF fighters in service became abundantly clear, and for many months ahead established itself as the fighter to be feared most in combat. Though a distinct shock to RAF higher authority, the Fw 190s obvious excellence vis-à-vis the Spitfire V needed a hasty remedy. An existing plan to bring together the Spitfire VII variant with a Merlin 61 engine had mooted a new fighter version, the Mark VIII, but Fighter Command requested an interim version which could be brought into operational use more quickly. The result was what amounted to a Mark Vc, powered by a Merlin 61, and designated Spitfire IX. Identifiable mainly by its twin radiators and four-bladed propeller, the Mark IX first entered service in July 1942 with 64 Squadron at Hornchurch and its first combat success was, appropriately, the destruction of a Fw 190 by Flight Lieutenant Don Kingaby on 30 July. The Merlin 61 of 1660hp had a two-speed supercharger and raised the Spitfire IXs top speed to slightly more than 400mph. Eventually the 'interim' Mark IX was built in greater quantity (5665) than any other Mark of Spitfire except the Mark V, and was still operational in 1945. It also introduced a fresh mixture of armament for the Spitfire – two 20mm cannons and two .50 machine guns, plus the capacity to lift an additional 1000lb bomb in the fighter-bomber role.

The marriage of Rolls-Royce Merlin engines to Spitfire airframes – a union which had been the kernel of success for the original design – continued in various other versions in other roles but the last significant fighter variant to use a Merlin was the Mark XVI, which was fitted with a Packard-built Merlin 266 of 1705hp (a license-built Merlin 66). Built in parallel with the earlier Mark IX, the XVI entered service in 1944, and a total of 1054 examples were finally constructed, the ultimate example being delivered in August 1945. In all 33 UK-based squadrons were eventually equipped with Mark XVIs, and others employed the type in various overseas theaters of the war. In performance and armament the XVI was almost identical to its Mark IX predecessor, and the XVI was to continue in service with the postwar RAF and Royal

Right: **Spitfire Mark XIV, RB140, first of a 50-aircraft batch built by Vickers-Armstrong (Supermarine) in 1943.**
Center Right: **A cheerful group of Polish pilots of 306 Squadron at Northolt in October 1942. The Spitfire is an FIXc, BS459, which was lost in action in January 1943.**
Below Right: **The answer to the Focke-Wulf Fw 190. Spitfire Mark IX s of 611 Squadron, AAF over a suburb in Kent in late 1942.**
Below: **Superb study of a Mark Vb, BL479, 'X-Ray' of the Polish 316 'City of Warsaw' Squadron.**

Left: Spitfire HF IX of an unidentified Free French squadron, taxying over snow-covered French ground in the winter of 1944-45. Note the French *tricolore* rudder stripes.
Below Left: Spitfire Mark XIV, the personal aircraft of Wing Commander Colin Gray, DSO, DFC, then Wing Leader at Lympne in late 1944, and sporting his initials.
Bottom: Mark XIVs of 610 'County of Chester' Squadron, AAF, led by Squadron Leader R A Newbury in DW-D, RB159, in September 1944.
Right: Beach-Head Servicing. RAF servicing commandos belting 20mm cannon shells on makeshift tables for the mixed batch of Spitfires behind, including Nos 56(US), 332(AH) and 411(DB) Squadrons; part of 2nd TAF, June 1944 for the Normandy invasion force.
Below: Mark LF XIVe, RW396 of the Central Gunnery School.

Auxiliary Air Force – the latter finally relinquishing their beloved Spitfires in 1951.

By 1943 the development potential of the Merlin engine had been exploited to the full, causing designers to search elsewhere for future fighter powerplants. One Rolls-Royce engine which had first commenced development prior to 1939 was the Griffon, like the Merlin a twelve-cylinder, sixty-degree 'Vee,' liquid-cooled engine, but of larger bore and stroke. Concentration upon the vast requirement for Merlin engines during the early war years – for virtually all types of RAF aircraft – had meant that the Griffon was temporarily shelved. In 1943 Luftwaffe fighters carrying bombs began a series of hit-and-run sneak raids in southern England, and the idea of a Griffon-engined Spitfire to counter such low-level raiders was proposed. The combination was successfully completed within weeks, resulting in the Spitfire Mark XII. Issued to just two units, 41 and 91 Squadrons at Hawkinge, and tasked solely with home defense duties, the Mark XII was rated to give its best performance at low levels, with its Griffon III or IV engine developing 1735hp at only 1000ft

altitude. Along with the brutish looking Hawker Typhoon, the Spitfire XII proved to be highly successful in tackling the high-speed Fw 190 sneak-raiders.

The potential of the Griffon engine opened fresh avenues for exploration of the Spitfire's development in various specialized roles. After the XII, the next significant version to be produced was the Mark XIV, powered by a Griffon 65 of 2050hp and intended for high-altitude interception roles. In outline the XIV had a longer nose and increased fin area compared to its elder brothers of the Spitfire family tree, and the more powerful engine drove a five-bladed propeller. A total of 957 Mark XIVs were built, and the type first entered

RAF service with 610 Squadron, AAF in January 1944. With its maximum speed nudging 450mph at over 25,000ft height, the XIV was the fastest RAF fighter in service on its introduction to operations, an asset which was exemplified from June 1944 when the first V-1 flying bombs began descending on southern England as the harbingers of Hitler's deliberate 'terror-weapons' assaults on the United Kingdom. Together with the sleek Hawker Tempest, Spitfire XIVs accounted for more than 300 of the cruciform robot bombs – some 75 percent of all V-1s claimed by UK-based Spitfire units. Other feats accomplished by Spitfire XIVs included a devastating three-squadron attack with bombs and cannons against V-2 rocket bases on 24 December 1944, and a claim by a 401 Squadron Mark XIV on 5 October 1944 for the first air victory over a German Messerschmitt Me 262 jet fighter. In addition to the home-based units, twenty squadrons of Spitfire XIVs served with the 2nd Tactical Air Force in France after June 1944, while the type began first-line service over Burma and India in early 1945.

If the Griffon engine undeniably stretched the Spitfire life-line superbly, to the purists its installation destroyed the classic beauty of the original Spitfire outline. Indeed, many Spitfire veterans have gone on record as saying that, with the Griffon engine, the Spitfire should have been renamed, thus preserving the nomenclature solely for the earlier Merlin-engined versions. There is undoubtedly strong support for such a view when one considers the relation of the Spitfire I to, say, the Mark F.21 which came into service in March 1945 but saw few war operations before VE Day. With its protruding lengthy snout, contra-rotating propellers, redesigned wing and tail forms, the F.21 bore only superficial resemblance to the '. . . most marvellous aircraft ever built.'

ACES AND KINGS

البحرين
BAHRAIN

1. Keith William 'Bluey' Truscott, DFC (right), the Australian ace, when serving with 452 Squadron in 1941. In 1942 he returned to Australia, saw further action, but died in a flying accident on 28 March 1943.
2. Wing Commander F D S Scott-Malden, DSO, DFC.
3. Squadron Leader Jean D F Demozay, DSO, DFC, a Frenchman who ran up a 21-victory tally before being killed in an accident on 19 December 1945.
4. J E 'Johnnie' Johnson, DSO, DFC, whose 38 claimed victories made him the highest-scoring RAF pilot in Europe.
5. Wing Commander W V 'Bill' Crawford-Compton, DSO, DFC the New Zealander who was credited with 22 victories.
6. From left, Squadron Leader Jack Charles, Commandant Rene Mouchotte, Group Captain A G Malan, and Squadron Leader A C Deere – taken on the date on which RAF Biggin Hill celebrated its 1000th claimed victory.

1. Adolph Gysbert 'Sailor' Malan, DSO, DFC, the legendary South African fighter leader, who finished the war with 35 victories. He died of Parkinson's disease in 1964.
2. Gregory Augustus 'Gus' Daymond, DFC (left) and Chesley Peterson, DSO, DFC, two of the Americans who served with 71 Squadron, the first 'Eagle' unit in the RAF, 1941.
3. Wing Commander Brendan Finucane, DSO, DFC (32 victories) seated in his 452 Squadron Spitfire, 1941. He was shot down into the Channel on 15 July 1942 and drowned.
4. Eric Stanley 'Sawn-Off' Lock, DSO, DFC (Bar) who fought through the Battle of Britain, but was killed during a daylight offensive sweep over France on 3 August 1941.
5. Squadron Leader Brian J E Lane, DFC, commander of 19 Squadron from September 1940, who claimed 16 enemy aircraft destroyed or damaged in 1940. He was killed in action in 1941.
6. Two 'Tiger' pilots of 74 Squadron in 1940. H M Stephen, DSO (left) and J C Mungo-Park, DFC. The latter died in action on 27 June 1941 over France.

ABOVE THE DESERT

From 11 June 1940 – the day after Italy's entry into the war – the tiny island of Malta was subjected to prolonged aerial attacks by the Italian *Reggia Aeronautica* and, later, the German Luftwaffe. The strategic location of Malta as a 'block' to the sea supply lines of enemy forces in the North African land war made it a vital base for the Allies to hold, and its aerial defense had assumed high priority by late 1941. Unfortunately, the demands of the European campaigns, Battle of Britain and the subsequent air offensive over occupied France *et al* precluded adequate reinforcement of Malta's pitifully thin air defenses until 1942. Until then the only modern fighters available to Malta pilots had been Hurricanes, which did trojan work but were clearly at a disadvantage when matched against some of the latest Italian and German fighters. The only real answer was to supply Spitfires to Malta, and in reasonable quantity. Only a single Spitfire had been seen in Malta during the year 1941, when Flight Lieutenant P Corbishley DFC set out from England in Spitfire PR (Photo-Reconnaissance) IV, P9551, to photograph Italian naval units in the Gulf of Genoa on 19 January. Blown off track, Corbishley decided to land at Malta and try again from there. On 2

February he set out again for Genoa but was hit by anti-aircraft fire, he baled out, and became a prisoner of war in Italy.

It was not until 7 March 1942 that the first Spitfire reinforcements for Malta actually arrived, incidentally, the first Spitfires to be sent to any overseas theater of war. These fifteen Spitfires flew off the aircraft carriers *Eagle* and *Argus* on Operation Spotter (code name for the reinforcement sortie).

Above: A Desert Air Force Mark Vb preparing for takeoff.
Far Left: Spitfire Vb, AB502, IR-G, the personal aircraft of Wing Commander Ian 'Widge' Gleed, DSO, DFC, marked with his 'Figaro' cat cartoon insignia, in which Gleed died in action on 16 April 1943.
Below Left: Spitfires became the turning point in the air siege of Malta. Seen here are Mark Vbs of 249 Squadron at Ta Kali airfield on Malta in early 1942.

They were Spitfire Vbs, each fitted with a Vokes filter under the nose to operate in the dusty and sandy conditions of the Mediterranean zone. A further sixteen Spitfires were flown off carriers later in March, but then, due to non-availability of British carriers, came a gap of a month before the Spitfire supply could be resumed. By borrowing the US carrier *Wasp*, a total of 54 Spitfires were embarked at Glasgow and on 20 April they took off from a point off Sardinia – though only 47 actually reached Malta. Within 48 hours enemy bomb attacks on the Maltese airfields had reduced this total to eighteen. On 9 May the *Wasp* and the *Eagle* flew off 64 more Spitfires, many of which were in action next day, claiming fifteen enemy aircraft shot down. Eight days later a further seventeen Spitfires flew in and the steady supply continued at intervals through June, July and August via various aircraft carriers, after which arrangements were put in hand for future reinforcements to fly direct from Gibraltar – a dead distance of almost 1400 miles. For this prodigious flight the Spitfires were fitted with 170-gallon gasolene tanks which could be jettisoned if need be. During November and December 1942 a total of fifteen Spitfires undertook the long haul across the Mediterranean and all except one reached Malta safely. These were the final reinforcements sent to the besieged island due to the favorable turn of the battles in North Africa in the Allies' favor.

The full story of the aerial war over Malta during the desperate years 1940–42 would require a separate book, but in primitive living and operational conditions, the fighter pilots in Malta fought against odds and in circumstances which led one veteran to remark, '. . . It all makes the Battle of Britain and fighter sweeps seem child's play in comparison.' From the siege came a host of names of outstanding Spitfire pilots, the most publicized being George 'Screwball' Beurling, a Canadian who ran up a tally of nearly thirty victories and was awarded a DSO, DFC and DFM in the same period. It would be totally false to claim that the arrival of Spitfires *ensured* ultimate victory in Malta, but their presence and prowess undoubtedly provided an enormous fillip to the morale of the weary and battered defenders and represented the balance between possible defeat and eventual triumph.

In the vaster war zones of North Africa the call for Spitfires

Below: A sunburned 601 Squadron AAF pilot and his Mark Vb in North Africa.

Above: **Springbok Spitfire of 2 Squadron, SAAF, No 7 SAAF Wing, with four 20mm cannons and 250lb GP bomb, patrolling over the Sangro River, Italy, 1944.**

was equally vociferous. The first unit to receive them was 145 Squadron in May 1942, who were sent Spitfire Vbs which first went into action on 1 June. By the end of August two more squadrons had re-equipped and the influx steadily increased. Other Spitfires to reach the Middle East theater included several PR IV variants allotted to No 2 PRU in Egypt, while at Aboukir a handful of Spitfire Vcs were specially stripped of every excess ounce of weight and had their engines artificially boosted. They were flown in several successful ultra-high altitude interception sorties against the Junkers Ju 86-P2 photo-reconnaissance aircraft which spied daily on Allied naval movements at the northern end of the Suez Canal. One of these 'high fliers,' piloted by Flight Officer G W H Reynolds, reached 50,000ft on one sortie, with Reynolds part-paralyzed by a cockpit temperature of 67 degrees below zero! In the desert campaigns the arrival of Spitfires was welcomed by the fighter pilots. The reaction of the Germans was possibly summed up in the words of Oberleutnant Werner Schoer of *Jagdgeschwader* 27 who scored 61 victories in Africa, 'The Spitfire arrived very late (in the campaign) but then the apprehension of our pilots was very great in memory of their experiences over the Channel. This fear was in many cases unfounded, because the excellent Spitfire needed an excellent pilot.' His reference to the lateness in sending Spitfires to the desert war is supported by Wing Commander G C Keefer, DSO, DFC who in 1942 was a Flight commander in 274 (Hurricane) Squadron, who recorded, 'Regarding the arrival of Spitfires, I can very well remember the first time we operated with them; . . . we had a top cover of two Spitfires from 145 Squadron and the feeling of comfort was tremendous. There is no question, whatsoever, in my mind that the earlier arrival of Spits in the desert would have made a vast difference in the air fighting.' (*Fighters over the Desert* by C F Shores & H Ring; Neville Spearman, 1969.)

Part of the reason for the slowness in re-equipping some desert units with Spitfires in 1942 was the gradual build up of aerial strength considered vital to support the forthcoming second front in Africa. Operation Torch, an Allied invasion of French-occupied North Africa, initially at Casablanca, Oran and Algiers, thus provided a pincer advance from the west which would eventually link up with the advancing Eighth Army from the east. Hundreds of Allied aircraft were shipped direct to Gibraltar, assembled and prepared for Torch in the late summer of 1942. Spitfires predominated in the wide variety of fighters assembled, not only in RAF squadrons but also in the American units allocated to the invasion forces. The main type of Spitfire used was the cannon-armed Mark V, suitably adapted to cope with desert conditions of operation. In the early hours of 8 November 1942 Torch commenced. Spitfires were prominent in the opening phases, and among the earliest units to fly in to freshly-captured airfields were 81 Squadron's Spitfire Vs at Maison Blanche. During the following months, in weather conditions of drenching rain and operating from mud quagmires barely recognizable as landing strips, the Spitfire squadrons flew intensive operations in support of the land forces' drive eastward.

Although the bulk of Spitfires supplied to Africa in the initial months were predominantly Mark Vs, in February 1943 No 72 Squadron was re-equipped with Mark IXs from Gibraltar, and within six months became the highest-scoring unit. The air war continued with the same intensity until the eve of victory; then on 13 May 1943, the last of the Axis forces in Africa formally surrendered. The North African war was over, and the Allied Service chiefs turned toward the next stage – the invasion of Sicily and, ultimately, the occupation of Italy. While many Western Desert pilots had grumbled at the lack of Spitfires for the North African fighting, by mid-1943 most RAF fighter units had either re-equipped, or were in the process of re-equipping with Spitfire Vs, VIIIs and IXs. The majority had also been modified to carry up to 1000lb of bombs under wings and fuselages in the latest fighter-bomber role. Later, such additional weaponry was supplemented by the fitting of 3in RP (Rocket Projectile) batteries under the wings for attacking armored vehicles, transport and installations in the path of the Allied infantry.

The invasion of Sicily commenced on 10 July 1943 and four days later 92 Squadron's Spitfire Vs and IXs made up the first unit to 'set up home' on the island, at Pachino. On 3 September the Allies set foot in the 'toe' of Italy as the advance rolled forward on the 'road to Rome.' Many Spitfire squadrons were among the aerial spearhead which blasted a path through enemy resistance for the British and American armies to follow. From then until the final cessation of hostilities, Spitfires were ubiquitous in their (mainly) support role; harrying and attacking every conceivable type of target throughout the Italian Campaign. Operating from makeshift patches of mud euphemistically referred to as 'airfields,' and under maintenance and flying conditions far removed from the sophisticated background originally considered necessary for the 'delicate' Spitfire, Mitchell's creation proved itself as tough as any other Allied fighter in such circumstances. Air opposition was small, compared to the fierce fighting in most other war zones, but

Above: **A pair of Spitfires of 241 Squadron over Italy.**

this hardly meant that the Spitfire units in Italy had a 'soft' war. Low-level strafing raids meant braving deadly, intense anti-aircraft fire from the retreating German army, a form of opposition which left few Allied aircraft unscarred.

In June 1944 the Balkan Air Force was formed, and Spitfires figured high in the equipment of such allies as Yugoslavia during subsequent operations. As the fighting areas moved further and further north, the borders of southern Germany came within striking range of Allied aircraft. In these circumstances a number of PRU Spitfires were ordered to photograph the enemy's homeland where, among other forms of opposition, they encountered occasional German jet fighters. Other roles for Spitfire fighter-bombers were the so-termed 'Cab Rank' sorties, whereby bomb-carrying Spitfires patrolled in sections above specified areas of the front-line fighting awaiting a radio call from an RAF ground liaison officer in the infantry's forward positions to direct them onto selected targets impeding the army's advance; a system of direct tactical support used so successfully in France during 1944–45 by (mainly) Hawker Typhoons. Whether operating low over the liquid mud of an Italian plain, or jinking through the rugged, rock-landscapes of the mountains, Spitfires undertook every task allotted to them without demur, and were in evidence on every fighting occasion until the final enemy surrender in northern Italy.

Inevitably, perhaps, the close of the war in Italy did not automatically mean a return to peaceful occupations by the Spitfire units in the Middle East zone. Britain still held bases in Egypt, by treaty, while the land of Palestine came under the UK's mandate for administration and control. The latter area had been in contention between the Jews and Arabs for many years, with the Jewish population struggling to establish their own state of Israel in defiance of Arab claims to the territory. Following a United Nations' agreement on a partition plan for the country, which came into effect in November 1947, Britain prepared to withdraw all her armed services by 15 May 1948. The interim period was marked by increasing hostility from both Jews and Arabs, each of whom was urgently rearming for the inevitable conflict to come once Britain had relinquished its control. Clashes between British troops and local dissidents mounted, with the Palestine-based Spitfire squadrons, Nos 32 and 208, supporting each British action. Retaliation took the form of attempts to sabotage aircraft based at Ein Shemer, where several machines were destroyed by bombs and explosive charges.

On 15 May 1948, two Spitfire LF IXs of the Royal Egyptian Air Force strafed Tel Aviv, losing one to machine-gun ground fire which later belly-landed on the nearby beach. Seven days later Ramat David, the base for Nos 32 and 208 Squadrons, was attacked by an unidentified Spitfire which bombed two of 32 Squadron's aircraft and destroyed them before escaping. Two hours later three more Spitfires attacked the airfield, but were intercepted by four of 208 Squadron's Spitfires which shot down two, while the third was shot down by RAF Regiment gunners guarding the base. All three were from the Egyptian air service. With the final evacuation of the British presence, the Jews declared Israel to be a state. Its air force's fighter arm comprised mainly Messerschmitt Bf 109s and Spitfires. Both types saw frequent combat in the ensuing Israeli–Egyptian conflict. While on 7 January 1949, four Spitfire FR XVIIIs of 208 Squadron, engaged in a border patrol reconnaissance from their base at Deversoir, Egypt, were all shot down by Israeli anti-aircraft guns and Spitfires, with one of 208's pilots being killed. These were the last combat casualties for RAF Spitfires in the Middle East, but Israel continued using the type until 1954, when more modern designs became available, and then sold 30 LF IXs and LF XVIs to the newly-independent Union of Burma. Replacements for 32 Squadron's Spitfires in the shape of Vampires were completed by May 1949; while 208 Squadron had changed from piston-engined Spitfires to jet-engined Meteors by March 1950.

Bottom: **Mark Vc of the 307th Fighter Squadron, 31st Fighter Group, 12th Air Force, USAAF in North Africa.**
Center: **Spitfire IXs of 208 Squadron from Ein Shemer, Palestine in 1947. The nearest carries an oblique-mounted camera next to the fuselage roundel.**
Below: **First Spitfire deliveries to North Africa were Mark Vbs; going initially to equip 145 Squadron at Helwan, Egypt, two of whose aircraft are seen here. Nearest is AB326 which had been shipped via Takoradi in West Africa.**

SEA BOOTS

Until mid-1943, when American-designed aircraft became generously available, the Fleet Air Arm's greatest deficiencies in aircraft types were in the fighter role. At the outbreak of war in 1939 the fighters in RAF use comprised a varied mixture of outdated designs, mainly of biplane configuration, and often merely 'navalized' variants of landplane fighters. The first single-seat monoplane fighter adopted by the FAA was the so-termed Sea Hurricane, which equipped 880 Squadron FAA in January 1941, and embarked on HMS *Furious* in the following July. Yet all Sea Hurricanes used subsequently were conversions of Hurricane land fighters; no Sea Hurricane was ever actually built as such. By 1942 sufficient quantities of Spitfires were being produced to permit a number to be allotted for FAA aircraft carrier use, and the initial testing, of a Spitfire Vb fitted with an arrester hook under its slim fuselage, had been undertaken by Commander H P Bramwell, DSO, DSC at the end of 1941 with what was at that time referred to as the Spitfire (Hooked) – a clumsy title soon changed to Seafire.

The original batch of 'Seafire 1bs' were in fact simply Spitfire Vbs with an additional, retractable V-frame arrester hook. Armament was usually twin 20mm cannons and four .303 Browning machine guns; though later Seafires were often fitted with wings carrying a four 20mm cannon battery instead. In June 1942 the first FAA unit to be Seafire equipped was 807 Squadron, which was joined aboard HMS *Furious* by the second Seafire unit, 801 Squadron – both units (and carrier) being earmarked for the forthcoming Operation Torch. In service the Seafire was patently superior in performance to the Sea Hurricane, but by no means as easy to operate from the pitching, narrow 'runways' of aircraft carriers at sea; its narrow track undercarriage and long engine cowling giving pilots a difficult test in pure pilotage. Equally, the initial batches of Seafire Is and IIs were not always easy to stow below decks on some carriers, as their fixed wings were too large for the elevating platforms normally used. With the introduction of the Seafire III, however, manually-folded wings were fitted which eased deck handling considerably, though at the same

Above: **Spitfire Vb, BL687, converted for deck landing as a Seafire Ib, with an arrester hook beneath the fuselage.**

Above: **A Seafire F.47 prototype, illustrating the rear-view canopy and more slender rear fuselage.**

time gave a 'folded' Seafire III a slightly comical 'Praying Mantis' appearance. All Seafire IIIs were also fitted with rocket-assisted takeoff (RATOG) equipment to ensure swift attainment of flying speed from a carrier deck.

The first operational use of Seafires came with Operation Torch – the invasion of North Africa – in November 1942, and Seafires were in action from soon after the invasion date, 8 November; with Sub-Lieutenant G C Baldwin, DSC of 807 Squadron FAA claiming a French Dewoitine D.520 fighter, shot down as the first-ever Seafire combat victory of the war. By the beginning of 1943 four more squadrons had received Seafires, mainly IIcs, and in that year ten more squadrons were fully or part-equipped with the type. The year 1943 saw Seafires in action during several assaults on enemy-occupied territories, in particular the Allied amphibious landing at Salerno in early September. For this invasion Seafires were often catapulted into the air from parent ships in order to save time in getting airborne, and many were lost during subsequent attempts to land back on the carriers – almost sixty in just five days of operations – leaving the naval 'V-Force' covering the landing operations with only 23 serviceable Seafires when it withdrew. Such a high loss rate due purely to accidents reflected the relatively 'delicate' nature of the Seafire in the context of sea-borne operational employment. The continual pounding effect on undercarriages and fuselages resulting from all carrier-deck landings often led to 'crinkle-back' distortion of the rear airframe, while the general rough-and-ready handling associated with all naval air operations required an extremely robust structure. The foul weather conditions and extremes of temperature on occasion were factors which had never been envisaged by the Spitfire's original design team. A further deficiency of the Seafire was its lack of adequate operational range for any extended escort duties with any carrier-launched strike force; a facet which was later to restrict Seafires in Pacific waters to Fleet-protection roles.

Above: The prototype Seafire III, MA970, with 'praying mantis' folding wings. This aircraft was later wrecked in a ground collision during test trials.
Left: Seafire F.47, PS948 taking off from HMS *Illustrious*.
Below: Prototype Seafire F.45, TM379 with Jeffrey Quil! at the controls. It was originally ordered to F.21 standard.

Above: The experimental Mark IXb, MJ892 during a test flight from Hamble, 1943.
Above Left: Seafire III, PP979 of 807 Squadron, FAA attempting to land aboard HMS *Hunter* in Pacific waters, 1945, and marked in contemporary SEAC roundels.
Below: FR47 Seafires aboard HMS *Triumph* of the 13th Carrier Air Group (800 Squadron, FAA) in mid-1949.

In 1944 Seafires were again prominent in the various Allied invasion assaults; in particular Operation Dragoon, the landings in southern France in August. Elsewhere in the Mediterranean theater Seafires were occasionally detached for land-based service with the Desert Air Force, mainly for tactical reconnaissance ('Tac-R') duties in support of the British Eighth Army's advance in Italy. Further north Seafires played a part in several of the aerial attacks on the German capital ship *Tirpitz* during the same year, mainly acting as fighter escorts to the torpedo and bomber strike formations, and claiming some Luftwaffe victims in combat. The utility of Seafires as Tac-R and general air 'observers' was exemplified in the Allied invasion of Europe commencing 6 June 1944. On that day, and for several weeks thereafter, four FAA squadrons (808, 885, 886 and 897) came under the aegis of the 2nd Tactical Air Force (2nd TAF) in No 34 (PR) Wing. Their duties included the novel role of 'spotting' for the heavy guns of the Royal Navy off-shore, pounding the German coastal gun emplacements overlooking the landing beaches.

At the turn of the year the emphasis on naval warfare was mainly concentrated in Far Eastern waters as the Allied navies began the final phases of attacking Japan and its outlying territories. A total of eight FAA squadrons were still equipped with Seafire IIIs – Nos 801, 807, 809, 879, 880, 887, 894 and 899 – all of which participated in the major operations covering the invasion of Rangoon and Penang, attacks on oil refineries in Sumatra, over the islands of Sakishima and Truk, and above the Japanese mainland. Of the twelve FAA squadrons still flying Seafires on VJ-Day (15 August 1945), eight were equipped with Merlin-engined Seafire IIIs. The remaining four, based in the UK and working up for Far East operations, had begun to receive Seafires with Griffon engines but saw no wartime action with these latest variants. The first Griffon-engined Seafire, designated Mark XV, was intended as a replacement for the older Seafire III, but the cessation of hostilities precluded any prolonged service. In May 1945 802 Squadron FAA received the first Seafire XVs, to be followed by Nos 803, 805 and 806.

During the first years of the peace further versions of Griffon-engined Seafires were phased into brief service with the Royal Navy and Royal Canadian Navy; the longest-lived variant being the Mark XVII; a development of the XV incorporating a 'bubble' canopy, greater fuel capacity and a provision in the FR-version for carriage of two F.24 cameras. Subsequent Marks of Seafire were, in the main, simply 'navalized' versions of the later Spitfire types. The ultimate Seafire variant was the Mark 47, a 'sea-version' of the Spitfire Mark 24. The Mark 47 first entered FAA service with 804 Squadron FAA in early 1948, and eventually part-equipped several other units in first-line service. One squadron to be sent Seafire 47s was No 800, FAA, which was equipped in April 1949, and at the end of that year commenced a series of active sorties against the Chinese 'bandits' in the Malayan Emergency – Operation Firedog – and employing 3in RP armament against jungle targets. In June 1950 the Korean War erupted, and 800 Squadron's Seafires – on board HMS *Triumph* – became the only Seafires to participate in the conflict; flying a total of 360 operational strikes and patrols. From 1951 Seafires were withdrawn from first-line squadrons and allotted to training units of the RNVR, and the latter eventually relinquished these in late 1954.

Although not intended for naval use, a spasmodic series of tests were undertaken to provide a float-version of the Spitfire for operations in coastal waters. The original idea was born during the disastrous Norwegian campaign of April 1940, and a standard Spitfire I, R6722, was fitted with a pair of

floats originally intended for conversion of a Blackburn Roc two-seat Fleet fighter. Trials showed pessimistic results, while the abrupt end to operations in Norway nullified the necessity for such a floatplane fighter. In 1942 the idea was tried again, when Spitfire Mk Vb, W3760 was fitted with floats of Supermarine design. Testing showed that the hybrid was highly maneuverable still, although maximum speed was reduced by some 30mph with the extra drag imposed by the 'sea boots.' Two further examples, EP751 and EP754, were converted under the official designation 'Experimental Aircraft No 181'; later a Spitfire LF IXb, MJ892 was also converted to a floatplane. In October 1943 the three Mark Vb converts were shipped in crates to Alexandria, Egypt, assembled and test-flown from the Great Bitter Lake; the eventual intention being to operate these as maritime fighters against German transport aircraft in the Aegean zone of operations. In the event German occupation of the possible bases for this trio prevented their use, and the scheme was cancelled. Pilots handling these three conversions recorded higher takeoff and landing speeds – by some 10–12mph – over the landplane Mark Vb equivalent. Apart from distinct tail-heavy characteristics which needed careful trim conditions in speed dives to avoid spinning tendencies, the 'Float-Spit' handled well. Its range in excess of 350 miles, and service ceiling of 33,000ft, promised well for the type had it ever been given an opportunity to fire its guns 'in anger.' By 1944, however, carrier-based fighters dominated tactical thinking and the need for a floatplane equivalent was considered most unlikely.

Bottom: Seafire F.15, PR479 of the 1st Training Group, Royal Canadian Navy at Dartmouth, Nova Scotia. Its call-sign VG-AAB, is painted on the underside of the wings.
Below: Seafire F.15, NS493, the third prototype, which was later modified to F.17 standard.

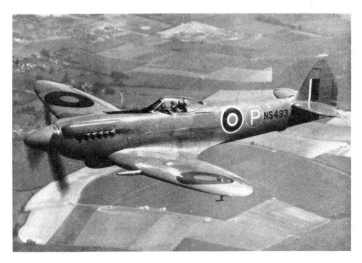

38

Above: **PR XI of 681 Squadron from Palem, India circa 1944 setting off on a photo-reconnaissance patrol.**
Left: **Spitfire LF VIII, MD351.**
Bottom: **A general view of the 'Spitfire' dispersal area on Bepingang Airstrip. Due to the limited amount of dispersal space, planes often had to be double parked in a small area.**
Below: **Spitfire F XVIII, TP377 over the Malayan jungle.**

OVER THE JUNGLE

With the entry of Japan into the war in December 1941, the Allied fighters then existing in the Far Eastern theater were a mixed batch of out-dated designs of hastily-converted aircraft intended for other roles. Far superior to any of these was the Japanese standard 'Zero' fighter, which was to hold its level of supremacy for the following two years. The first Spitfires to reach the Far East were two PR IVs (BP911 and BP935) in October 1942, which were then allotted to No 2 PRU, and within nine days began photo-reconnaissance sorties over Japanese-held areas. Meanwhile the obvious threat of Japanese invasion of northern Australia caused the Allies to begin a build up of aerial strength there. In June 1942 No 54 Squadron RAF was sent overseas to an unspecified destination, with its Spitfire Vcs crated, only to have the aircraft diverted to the Mediterranean zone, and the unit personnel sent on to South Africa to await further orders. By January 1943 the squadron had become based in Richmond, New South Wales, and was part of a newly-forming fighter Wing, No 1, RAAF, composed of 54 Squadron RAF and Nos 452 and 457 Squadrons, RAAF. Wing equipment was the Spitfire Vc, and all three squadrons were sent to Darwin on the Australian northwest coast. Combat was soon forthcoming, and on 6 February Flight Lieutenant Bob Foster of 54 Squadron shot a Japanese Type 100 Ki-46 'Dinah' into the sea – the first Spitfire kill against Japanese aircraft.

Led in the air by Wing Commander Clive 'Killer' Caldwell, DFC, No 1 Wing saw constant action in defense of the Darwin area until September 1943, after which Japanese assaults on the Australian continent virtually petered out. By August 1943 the Wing's tally alone of victories stood at 64 destroyed and more than thirty others damaged or probably destroyed. These successes had not been without loss, however. While a Spitfire Vc could always outspeed a Zero, in the tight dogfight maneuverability context there was little to choose between the two aircraft, and Spitfire tactics were usually a high-speed diving attack followed by a fast breakaway climb. By 1944 it was possible to form further Australian Spitfire squadrons, including Nos 548 and 549 which joined 54 Squadron in the defense of northern Australia. Their predecessors, Nos 452 and 457 were then combined with 79 Squadron RAAF to form 78 Wing, and this unit was dispatched to the New Guinea area for further front-line operations. By April 1944 54 Squadron began re-equipping with Spitfire VIIIs, but remained in Australia until disbandment in November 1945.

In the India/Burma Theater of operations the need for Spitfires to combat the Zero was paramount, but it was not until September 1943 that the first Spitfire Vs were collected from the Karachi depot by pilots of 605 and 615 Squadrons, to exchange for their battered Hurricanes. On 4 October came 615's first Spitfire 'scramble,' but the first victory did not occur until 8 November when a Dinah was sent down in flames. It was the start of the long road back to Allied air superiority over Burma; an ascendency directly attributable to the impact of the Spitfires upon the aerial war. If the Mark Vc was only marginally better than its best opponents, the arrival of the Mark VIIIs by March 1944, which by then equipped a total of eight squadrons, offered an unqualified advantage in all sections of the performance envelope. Powered by a 1520hp Merlin 61, with a top speed in excess of 400mph, the Mark VIII had first seen Burma service with 155 Squadron

Above: **Spitfire FR XIVe of 273 Squadron, based at Saigon, escorting ACM Sir Keith Park (AOC-in-C, SEAC) to Singapore, 1945.**

Above: **Spitfire XVIII of 60 Squadron at Tengah, Singapore during Operation Firedog.**

from November 1943, and by mid-1944, when fitted with additional 45-gallon fuel tanks, was capable of long-range escort and strafing sorties in the Japanese hinterland areas.

The conditions, with which all air crews had to contend, over the matted Burma jungle were part-exemplified by a tragic formation sortie by sixteen Spitfires of 615 Squadron on 10 August 1944. En route to Calcutta the formation flew into cumulonimbus clouds and within seconds each pilot was fighting for his life as the strong winds tossed the Spitfires about like so many paper toys. Eight of the formation were lost and four of the pilots killed. The pilots of the remaining Spitfires barely managed safe landings having suffered a considerable buffeting. By then the superiority of Spitfires over anything flown by the Japanese had become evident. During the battle for the Imphal Valley earlier in 1944, Spitfires had played an important part in the eventual triumph. The 607 Squadron alone claimed 47 Japanese aircraft destroyed or badly damaged during a twelve-week run of successes.

During the last year of the war, combat with Japanese aircraft became less frequent, and the Spitfire squadrons were mainly employed as escorts for the patient Dakota crews maintaining air supply to the jungle-bound infantry; or more frequently in the low-level strafing role. The latter form of sortie offered a wide variety of targets – gunning every conceivable form of road and river transportation in use by a steadily retreating Japanese army. Another feat, seldom given due publicity, was the extraordinary efforts of the photo-reconnaissance squadrons – mainly DH Mosquitos, but including 681 Squadron, equipped with Spitfires. Ranging far and wide the PRU air crews were able to put on film details of possible targets and objectives as far afield as Sumatra, Java

and Singapore. From the early part of 1944 they eventually produced a complete photographic survey of Burma itself – a country which at that time was ill-served by existing maps. All these sorties were undertaken in weather conditions which, at times, could only be described as 'discouraging.' The unbridled power of nature at its worst was illustrated starkly to a New Zealand Warrant Officer pilot, F D C Brown, of 681 Squadron, when returning to Chittagong from a PR sortie in June 1943. Flying at 23,000ft he found himself confronted with a cloud wall extending in every visible direction, leaving him no alternative but to attempt to fly through it. The next twenty minutes grew rougher and rougher as his Spitfire was bumped and shaken alarmingly by internal cloud currents. Then a sudden series of harsh bumping threw the aircraft into a tight spin, pinning Brown in his seat with increasing g forces until he fell unconscious. 'When I came to' he reported later, 'I was falling head over heels just under the cloud base, with pieces of the aircraft fluttering all around me and the main part of the fuselage two or three hundred feet below me, minus the engine, wings and tail unit. . . .'

In 1944 Spitfire XI PR-variants began to re-equip some photo-reconnaissance units in India. In early 1945 a batch of Mark XIVs were received in India and eventually equipped Nos 17 and 132 Squadrons before the war with Japan ended. These improved-performance Spitfires, though welcomed, were hardly needed by then. Mastery over the Japanese air services was already virtually complete, thanks to the original introduction of Spitfires to the jungle war – an event described in one official history; '. . . the advent of the Spitfire squadrons brought promise of victory as the arrival of the swallow that of summer.' In August 1945 two atomic bombs devastated selected cities on the Japanese mainland, Hiroshima and Nagasaki. Shortly afterward the Emperor decided

Below: **Spitfire VIIIs of 136 Squadron in the Cocos Islands, 1945.**

Above: **Spitfire F.24, PK682 of B Flight, 80 Squadron from Kai Tak, Hong Kong in August 1950.**

Above: **Mark XIX, PS888 of 81 Squadron at Seletar, Singapore – the aircraft which flew the last RAF Spitfire 'war flight' on 1 April 1954.**

to surrender and within days the war in the Far East was officially declared to be over.

The advent of 'peace' in the Far East was hardly noticeable among RAF squadrons based there in mid-1945. Relieved of the yoke of Japanese occupation, many former French, Dutch and British 'colonies' chose this opportunity to assert nationalistic ambitions, refusing to merely resume colonial status for the various European prewar 'masters.' In French Indo-China the revolt against the former administration erupted into military defiance, which involved a number of French Spitfire LF IXs. In the Dutch East Indies, defiance of its former Dutch 'owners' took the shape of proclaiming a new state named Indonesia, and wide preparation to resist any attempts to reimpose Dutch control. Caught in the middle of the latter revolution were the British servicemen who were trying to repatriate their countrymen from former Japanese prisoner-of-war camps, and at the same time rounding up and disarming resident Japanese forces in the area. Clashes with rebel forces finally brought the RAF into direct action, including 155 Squadron's Spitfires which saw brief combat and carried out several ground strikes, before finally withdrawing to the British base at Singapore.

Throughout Malaya, meantime, Chinese Communists, who had fought alongside the Allies against the Japanese during the war, now commenced a campaign of terrorism and murder to weaken and eventually overthrow British colonial control of the country. In May 1948 a state of emergency was declared, and what became known as Operation Firedog came into being: a prolonged battle against these 'bandits' (sic) which was to last twelve years. Already based in Malaya at that period were two Spitfire squadrons, Nos 28 and 60, and these were soon in action; strafing suspected bandit hideouts in the jungle with guns, cannons and rockets. Both squadrons were

equipped with Spitfire FR.18s – aircraft with performance ranges comparable with the early Marks of Meteor and Vampire jet fighters which had begun to re-equip UK-based fighter units. In 1949, 28 Squadron's Spitfires were flown to Hong Kong as a precaution against possible investment of that colony by Chinese communists across the nearby border. They were joined there by 80 Squadron, fresh from Germany and equipped with Spitfire F.24s.

Backing the strike squadrons in Malaya was 81 Squadron, based at Seletar airfield, operating a mixture of Mosquito PR34s and Spitfire PR XIXs in the photo-reconnaissance role. On occasion 'outside' assistance from non-resident RAF and FAA units was given as the opportunity arose. An example of the latter occurred on 19 December 1949 when strikes against bandit strongholds were flown by, among others, Seafires from HMS *Triumph*. On 2 December 1950, however, six Vampire F5 jet fighters arrived in Singapore. They were the first jets in the Far East Air Force and were flown in as the initial re-equipment for 60 Squadron. The ultimate Spitfire operational sortie by 60 Squadron was flown on 21 January 1951, and by April the unit had commenced Vampire sorties. Despite wide press publicity about this 'last Spitfire sortie,' 81 Squadron continued to operate its PR XIXs until 1 April 1954, on which date 81 Squadron's commander, Squadron Leader W P Swaby, flew Spitfire PS888 on what was indeed the Spitfire's ultimate 'war flight.' Even then Spitfires elsewhere were to continue on war-like operations for a few months; these being some thirty Mark LF IXs purchased from Israel by the newly-independent Burma which were employed in ground strikes against dissidents.

Below: **Spitfire FXIVes of 28 Squadron at Kuala Lumpur, Malaya in 1946. 'T' is SM893, and 'H' is NH869.**

Above: Spitfire Vb, BM635 of the USAAF 67th Observation Group, based at Membury, but still retaining the identity coding of its previous 'owners,' the 309th Fighter Squadron, USAAF. Seen here on 15 March 1943.
Top: Spitfire PR VII, illustrating the 'blister' canopy and fuselage port for an oblique-view camera.
Above Left: A much-modified Spitfire Mark I, L1004, in its guise as the prototype Mark XIII PR variant. Note the camera port near roundel.
Left: PRU Spitfire leaving a contrail at 30,000ft.
Bottom Left: Alistair Lennox Taylor, DFC, the pioneer photo-reconnaissance pilot who was the first RAF officer of World War II to receive two Bars to his DFC. He was killed in action on 4 December 1941.
Below: A Mark VII Merlin 4.5 seen in May 1943.

EYES IN THE SKY

The value of photographic reconnaissance became recognized as early as 1911, during the brief Italian–Turkish war in Libya, and indeed aerial photography can be traced as far back as the late nineteenth century. During the 1914–18 war the use of the aerial camera became widespread by all participating nations, yet in the postwar 'locust years' of the RAF little was done to change and improve equipment – particularly aircraft – toward expansion and improvement of such aerial intelligence. By 1939, with war only a few months away, a photo-reconnaissance unit was finally established at Heston, 'commanded' by the unorthodox photo-genius Sidney Cotton. With the outbreak of war the RAF's need for aerial intelligence became urgent, and Cotton experimented with various types of aircraft for PR work, but finally concluded that only a fast Spitfire could efficiently fulfill the role. Frustrated by refusals to let him have a Spitfire by other authorities, Cotton finally saw ACM Sir Hugh Dowding, Air Officer Commanding-in-Chief, Fighter Command in October 1939, and boldly requested two Spitfires. Dowding's response was to have two sent to Heston the following morning. Both aircraft were ruthlessly stripped of all excess weight, including armament, and had all external surfaces smoothed into a hard, sleek gloss finish, thereby raising the Spitfires' top speed to almost 400mph. Then an F.24 camera was installed in each wing, and the whole airframe painted in a pale duck-egg green 'Camotint' finish for 'invisibility.'

On 5 November one Spitfire and its crew was 'detached' to Seclin, France, from where on 18 November Flight Officer M V Longbottom took off on the first-ever PR sortie by a Spitfire (N3071), bound for Aachen – although in the event bad weather forced him to abort the sortie. Between then and 10 January 1940 'Shorty' Longbottom completed fifteen sorties, on ten of which he was able to return with photographs covering some 5000 sq miles of enemy territory. He had also, incidentally, clearly demonstrated that PR results would be best obtained in a fast, unarmed fighter relying on speed to outwit any opposition, rather than any ability to fight back. This principle was adhered to in all further RAF photo-reconnaissance work. During early 1940 the PR organization at Heston expanded, recruiting pilots like Eric le Mesurier, Alistair Taylor and S G 'Billy' Wise, men who were to achieve huge success in this new specialized form of aerial warfare. On 18 June 1940 the Heston unit was officially placed under the aegis of No 16 Group, Coastal Command, with Wing Commander Geoffrey Tuttle, DFC as its new commander. By then the unit owned a total of eleven Spitfires – eight Mark PR 1bs and three PR 1cs. (The designations of these early PR Spitfires as Mark 1 is actually retrospective; originally they were titled simply as Spitfires 'A', 'B', 'C' et al.) The PR 1c was the first Spitfire to incorporate a fuselage camera mounting, and the 'blister'-modified cockpit canopy associated with nearly all future PR Spitfires. On 27 December 1940, to avoid possible

Above: **Spitfire PR XIX, PS853 taxying out.**

destruction by bombing of its base headquarters at Heston, the PRU was moved to Benson in Oxfordshire.

This first year of PR operations by Spitfires produced a number of progressive modifications and innovations based on the hindsight of experience. Much thought was given to the question of 'camouflage' finishes to render the high-flying Spitfires inconspicuous, if not exactly invisible, to enemy eyes. After Cotton's initial duck-egg green livery, various paint schemes were mooted and tested, but eventually the general consensus of opinion favored a deep blue, officially labelled 'PR Blue,' overall finish for high altitude work in the sub-stratosphere. Low-level reconnaissance machines were given a pink paint scheme. With the introduction of the so-termed Type 'D' equipment standards, that is, two cameras fitted in the fuselage, and wing fuel tanks of 66.5 gallons capacity each, plus a host of pilot 'comfort' items such as oxygen, heating etc, a Spitfire Mark V was modified to accept the 'D' equipment and became known as the Spitfire PR IV. In all 229 PR IVs were produced, and the type was still in operational use at the end of the war. Different equipment specified as the 'E' and 'F' standards (mainly different camera installations) also came within the PR IV category of Spitfire.

Between 1940 and 1945 a number of further PR versions of the Spitfire were produced. Most of these were hybrids of existing standard Marks of the type, but designated with Mark numbers which tend to create some confusion in specific identification by type. For example, the PR VII (or Type 'G'), basically an armed version of the PR IV, was in reality simply a modified variant of the standard Mark V – not, as may be thought logically, a PR-version of the standard Spitfire FVII. Again, its main successor, the PR X was in fact developed from the standard Mark XI and, indeed, *followed* the Mark XI into production. Introduced into service in May 1944, only sixteen examples were built and these differed from predecessors on the PR scene by having pressurized cockpit 'cabins.' The Mark XI itself was an adaptation of the Mark IX and a total of 471 PR XIs were eventually produced and saw RAF service until at least 1947, while three PR XIs sold to Denmark after the war continued in service until mid-1955. As with almost all PR Spitfires, the PR XI was unarmed, relying on its top speed of more than 400mph at height to elude opposition. It was also the first PR-variant to have a negative-g carburetor fitted during the production stage.

Last of the line of PR Spitfires produced was the PR XIX, the sole Griffon-engined version employed on such duties. Even this type remained a hybrid, having a late production standard Mark XIV airframe adapted to a Mark Vc wing with extra fuel tankage, and camera installations harking back to the PR IV. Developed in early 1944, the PR XIX was powered by a Griffon 66 (Griffon 65 on the first twenty examples produced) which gave it a top speed of almost 450mph at 26,000ft, and an optimum range – with overload fuel tankage – of 1455 miles. Brought into RAF service from May 1944, a total of 225 PR XIXs were built and the bulk of these featured pressurized cockpits. Longest-lived of all PR Spitfires, the PR XIX had been 'designed' particularly with the needs of the India/ Burma war in mind, and it was perhaps very appropriate that the final flight by an operational PR XIX was from Seletar, Singapore on 1 April 1954 – the final Spitfire flight in first-line service for the RAF.

Although no longer sporting RAF cockades, the PR XIX continued in everyday use in civilian garb until 1957 in the United Kingdom. In April 1951 a civilian THUM (Temperature and Humidity) unit was formed at Hooton Park, contracted by Air Ministry to provide daily meteorological observations of the upper atmosphere, that is, above 30,000ft. Three PR XIXs were used for this task, and three months later the unit moved to Woodvale, Lancashire. For the next six years, flown by civilian pilots, the 'Met-Spits' completed more than 4000 such flights. One pilot, John Formby, accumulated a total of 1400 flying hours during the course of 840 Met sorties in Spitfires – probably a record in the context of the design's history. This unpublicized saga of routine, yet on occasion dangerous, Spitfire duties finally ended in June 1957 when the faithful 'Spits' were replaced by Mosquitos. Flown in all weather conditions in an airplane never designed for high intensity instrument flying, these 'weather trips' were a tribute to both aircraft and pilots.

Above: **A Mark IX modified for photo-reconnaissance with the South African Air Force.**
Top: **PR XIX, PS925 of the PRU.**

Above: **Loading PR XIX, PM620 of 2 Squadron, RAF with a pair of long-focus F52 cameras, post-1945.**
Below: **PR XI, PL775, 'A' of 541 Squadron, Benson in 1944, wearing full 'invasion' striping.**

Above: **The Spitfire PR VII prototype, AB450, with pointed wing-tips when serving with the High Altitude Flight at Northolt, 1942.**

FAREWELL TO WINGS

Above: F.21, LA195 of 615 'County of Surrey' Squadron RAuxAF.
Below: No 2 Squadron, RAF in 1949. On the left are its Spitfire FR XIVs (A Flight), and on the right PR XIXs (B Flight).

While all Merlin-engined versions of the Spitfire and Seafire saw some degree of operational service during the years 1939–45, the Mark F.21 Griffon-engined Spitfire was the last of its ilk to enter front-line RAF service before the Japanese surrender in August 1945. The Mark XIV first equipped 610 Squadron, AAF, in January 1944, joining the home-based defenses against the German V-1 flying bombs from June of that year. Its effectiveness as a high performance, high-altitude fighter was exemplified on 5 October 1944 when a 401 Squadron RCAF pilot claimed the destruction of the first Messerschmitt Me 262 jet fighter to be shot down by the Allies, the first of many Luftwaffe pilots to reach Valhalla through a Spitfire's gunsight. Following the Mark XIV into production came the Mark XVIII; a redesign incorporating a bubble canopy hood, increased fuel tankage, and strengthened airframe to accommodate the extra all-round weight. It was built in two main versions, as a day fighter and a fighter-reconnaissance, with provision for stowage of up to three cameras, though still retaining a standard Mark XVIII's armament of twin 20mm Hispano cannons and a brace of .50 machine guns, plus possible carriage of 1000lb of bombs. Total production of the Mark XVIII was 300 machines, two-thirds of these being the fighter-reconnaissance variant, and these equipped squadrons overseas in the immediate postwar years.

By 1944 the development potential of the basic Spitfire design was reaching its pinnacle, and in that year the airframe underwent a major redesign. Built exclusively at the Castle Bromwich factories, the resulting Spitfire F.21 bore only a superficial resemblance to Mitchell's original pleasing shaping. Gone was the characteristic elliptical wing planform, being replaced by an angular outline built to house four 20mm cannons. The nose section had been further stretched to accommodate either a Griffon 61, 65 or 89; the tail and fuselage had been redesigned and substantially strengthened; 190lb of armor plating was installed, metal-covered rudders and many other minor details incorporated. The change was so great that at first it was thought necessary to retitle this latest development the Supermarine Victor, but it finally emerged as the F.21. With its empty weight topping 7000lb, the F.21 was the heaviest version of the Spitfire built to date, and subsequent pilots quickly came to realize the difference in handling, especially at takeoff and landing; the wider track and slightly taller undercarriage – necessary to account for an 11ft diameter propeller – feeling strange to veteran Spitfire pilots.

The F.21 was tested at the Air Fighting Development Unit late in 1944 and its resulting report was decidedly scathing, including the view, '. . . the control characteristics are such that this aircraft is most difficult to fly accurately and compares most unfavorably with other modern fighters.' The same report concluded most emphatically that the Mark XIV was a far superior fighter in virtually all respects. Notwithstanding such calumny, the F.21 entered RAF service in March 1945 with 91 Squadron, which commenced F.21 operations the following month from Ludham, Norfolk, flying armed reconnaissance patrols off the Dutch coastline. On 26 April two pilots of the squadron discovered and destroyed a German midget submarine of the six-ton *Biber* type near the Hook

– virtually the only victim of F.21 operations during the closing weeks of the war. Mass-production orders for 3000 F.21s were placed; in the event only 122 examples were actually built and these saw limited service with the RAF.

From the F.21 design came two more distinct Spitfire versions, the F.22 and F.24. Both had rear-view bubble canopies and more slender rear fuselages than the F.21, but in most other respects differed only in minor details. Production of F.22s commenced in March 1945 but only 260 were eventually built. These equipped only one RAF regular unit, 73 Squadron in Malta, but twelve Royal Auxiliary Air Force squadrons were re-equipped with the type, thereby giving the Spitfire a renewed lease of flying life wearing RAF roundels. Though little used by the RAF, several batches of F.22s were acquired by the Rhodesian and Syrian air forces, and a handful were flown by the Royal Egyptian Air Force. In RAuxAF service, the F.22 achieved one very minor claim to fame, being one of the very few Spitfires of any type to wear colored unit markings – as per the pre-1938 RAF markings – on overall silver paint finishes.

The ultimate Mark of Spitfire ever built – the F.24 – was in essence an F.22 with modifications. It had an increased range and incorporated the necessary facilities under the wing for addition of rocket projectiles. Production of the F.24 was restricted to 54 examples and some of these entered RAF service in November 1946. Three years later a batch of sixteen re-equipped 80 Squadron for service in Hong Kong, based at Kai Tak. Operating for the next two years in relatively rough maintenance and flying conditions, 80 Squadron's pilots found the F.24 a basically stable fighter, and once its highly sensitive control response and high power were understood and mastered, an exhilarating aircraft to fly. Compared to contemporary Meteor and Vampire jets, the F.24 had a limiting speed 0.15 Mach higher, with a service ceiling and speed at height superior to the Meteor, Vampire, Phantom I or Lockheed F-80. It could outmaneuver any contemporary fighter it met, yet offered its pilots the same basic gentleness in stall or spin as that of its illustrious predecessors. At the beginning of 1952 the squadron was finally re-equipped with De Havilland Hornets, and handed its F.24s to the Hong Kong Auxiliary Air Force, which continued using them for another three years.

One interesting development from the Spitfire which commenced in production just prior to the end of the war was the Supermarine Spiteful. Ordered to Air Ministry Specification F.1/43, the Spiteful employed a radically new form of laminar-

Above: A Mark F.24, the last variant, viewed in October 1946.
Top: A Mark 21 of the Central Fighter Establishment.
Right: Spitfire F.22, virtually identical to the F.21 except for the bubble canopy and slimmer rear fuselage.

flow thin wing of angular appearance, had a much larger tail fin and rudder than any predecessor and was fitted with an inward-folding undercarriage. Last of the line of Supermarine piston-engined fighter designs, the Spiteful was powered by a Griffon 69, 89, 90 or 101 with either three-blade contra-rotating or single five-blade propellers, giving it a maximum speed of almost 500mph (408mph at sea level). Armament comprised four 20mm cannons in the wings, and provision for the carriage of up to 2000lb of bombs, or a rocket projectile battery under the wings. Only seventeen Spitefuls were manufactured, four of these being taken on RAF charge for Service evaluation but none seeing squadron service. A 'navalized' version of the Spiteful – titled Seafang – appeared in early 1946, but again production was limited to merely eighteen aircraft, none of which entered front-line service. In its final F.32 version the Seafang incorporated wings which could be folded upward by hydraulic control actuated from the cockpit when the engine was running.

Below: LF XVIes of 501 Squadron, RAuxAF during an annual exercise.

Actual production of Spitfires eventually ceased on 20 February 1948 when the ultimate factory-fresh machine was delivered. In all a total of 20,351 Spitfires and 2408 Seafires had rolled from manufacturers' assembly lines since June 1936. If the Spitfire had completed its faithful service to the RAF by the early 1950s, a host of overseas countries continued to want Spitfires for reconstitution of their own air services. France, South Africa and Belgium each equipped squadrons with the type, while Belgium still had some 120 Spitfires on its air force's strength in mid-1952. Although a few Spitfires had reached Canada during the war, it was with Seafires that the Canadian Navy armed its air service in the immediate post-1945 era.

Spitfires had seen service in every campaign of the war, by land, sea and air, and had been the major fighter of a dozen air forces. In their cockpits had sat men from almost every nation in the world. For several thousands of young men a Spitfire had been their last earthly link with life. During the 1950s and early 1960s more than 100 Spitfires were preserved as examples of this splendid little fighter in Britain alone. Some forty of these served as gate guardians near the main entrances of a variety of RAF stations and other Service establishments – reminders to younger generations of the prowess and sacrifices of their elders. Today (1980) less than fifty remain, largely in national museums around the globe, or lovingly restored in civil or pseudo-Service livery by private owners. Fittingly the Royal Air Force continues to maintain a 'Battle of Britain Flight' – a small but excellent stock of flying Spitfires and Hurricanes – which are used sparingly for particular fly-over salutes each September as the British nation (among others) commemorate the 'Few'. They also thrill today's youngsters at air shows and exhibitions, while for older generations the silk-like drumming and whistle of a Merlin engine combined with the incredible beauty of sleek elliptical wings, flashing diamond-like in the bright sunlight, signifies only one name – Spitfire. As the distinguished painter Sir William Rothenstein once described the aircraft, it was '. . . as pretty and as precious looking as a cavalier's jewelled rapier.'

Above: **Spitfire IX of 1 Squadron, South African Air Force in 1947. Note the RP stubs and bomb carriers under the wings.**
Top: **Photo-reconnaissance XIX, PM577, one of Woodvale's meteorological Spitfires, after a winter THUM sortie.**
Top Right: **The Supermarine Spiteful, RB515 with the laminar-flow wing.**
Below: **Ex-photo-reconnaissance XIX, PS875 in Swedish Air Force markings as '60' of 1st Division of F11, SAF.**

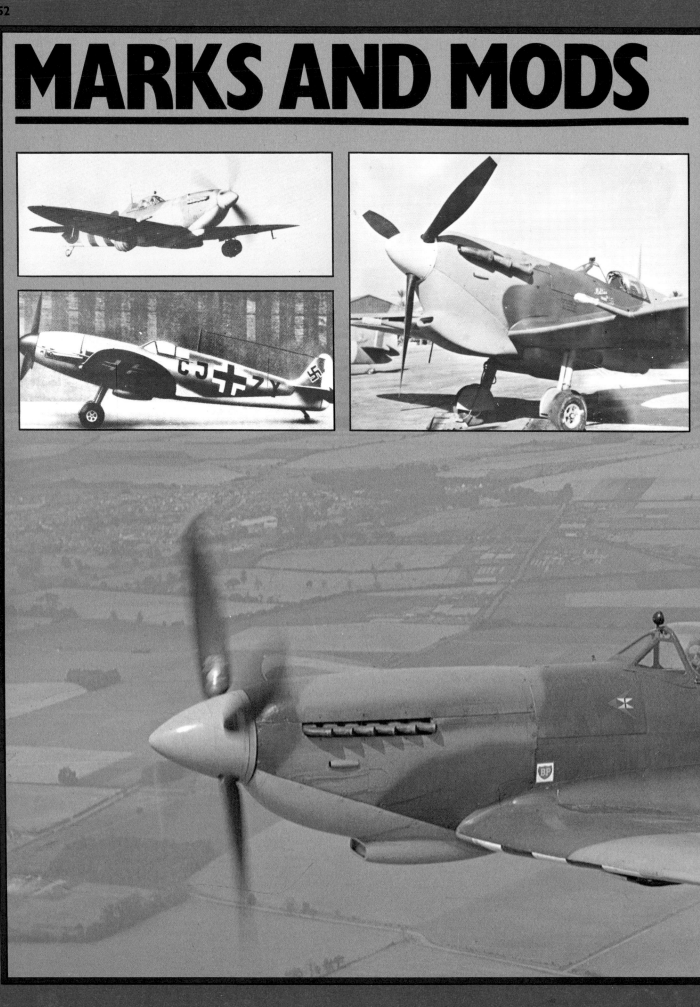

MARKS AND MODS

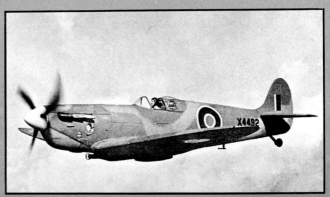

Above: Mark Vc, BR202 under trials with a 170-gallon ferry tank and enlarged nose oil tank.
Top Right: Spitfire Mark IX, photographed on 13 May 1944, with 'overload' wing tanks.
Right: Spitfire X4492, originally built as a Mark I, which served with No 1 PRU, then RAF Benson, before being sent to Canada for photo-reconnaissance duty. On 9 July 1945, piloted by Flight Lieutenant T Percival (as here), a total eclipse of the sun was photographed, in company with N A Mitchell 891.
Left: A Mark V with the 'desert' nose filter modification.
Far Left Top: A Mark IX modified to carry two beer barrels to invasion forces in Normandy, summer 1944.
Far Left Center: A Mark Vb, EN830 after its capture by the Luftwaffe and conversion to a Daimler-Benz DB601A engine.
Below: A superb flying shot of a Mark IX, MH434 with the late Neil Williams at its controls.

1. Spitfire LF IXc, MK304, Y2-K of 442 Squadron RCAF undergoing an engine change in the field.
2. An 80 Squadron machine has a propeller servicing at Kai Tak, Hong Kong, 1950.
3. Spitfire DP845, one of two prototypes ordered in 1941 to basic design, then strengthened and modified for testing engines under development by Rolls-Royce.
4. A two-seat conversion for civil use, G-AIDN, a TR8 variant.
5. The distinctive clipped-wing of a Mark Vb Spitfire.
6. A Mark IXe, loaded with one 500lb and two 250lb GP bombs, with Wing Commander Geoffrey Page, DFC in the cockpit in France 1944.

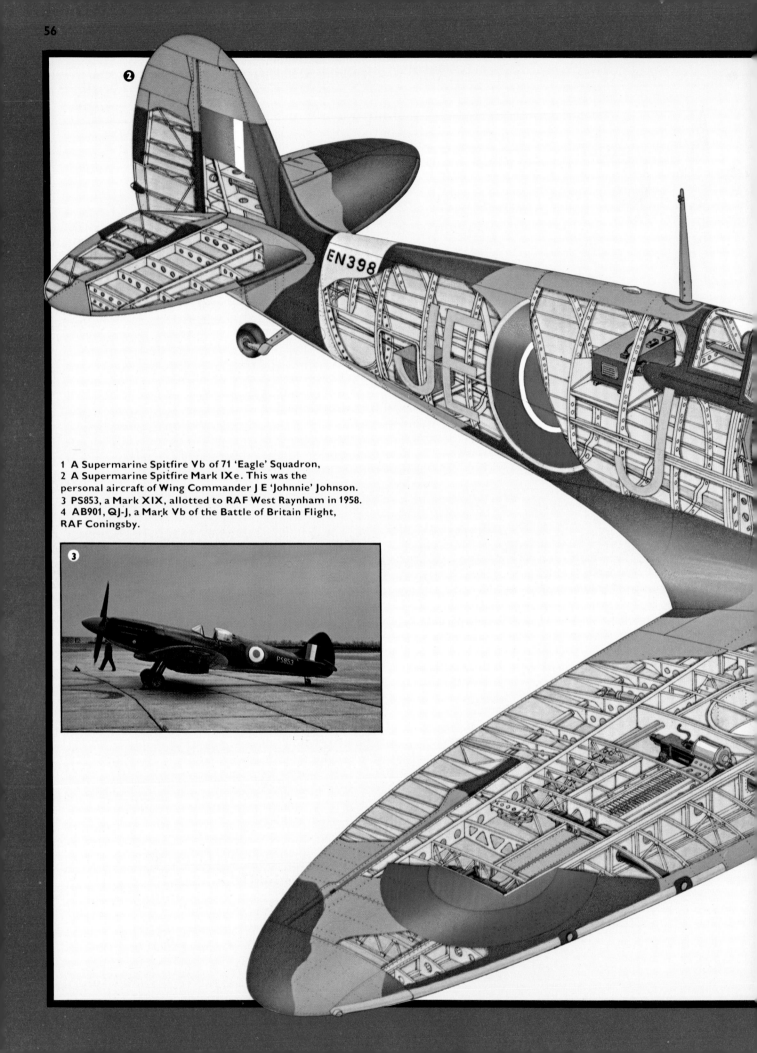

1 A Supermarine Spitfire Vb of 71 'Eagle' Squadron,
2 A Supermarine Spitfire Mark IXe. This was the
personal aircraft of Wing Commander J E 'Johnnie' Johnson.
3 PS853, a Mark XIX, allotted to RAF West Raynham in 1958.
4 AB901, QJ-J, a Mark Vb of the Battle of Britain Flight,
RAF Coningsby.

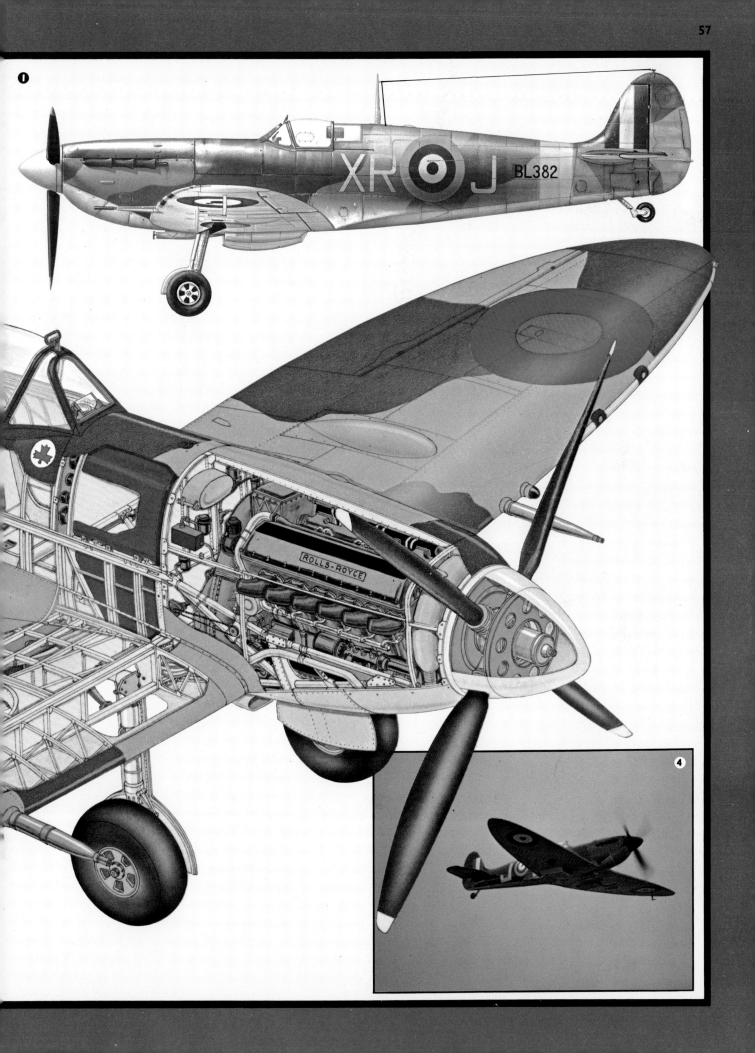

Left and Above: Spitfires in production. Over 6000 Spitfire Vs alone were produced during the war. The work was subcontracted to many factories throughout Britain.

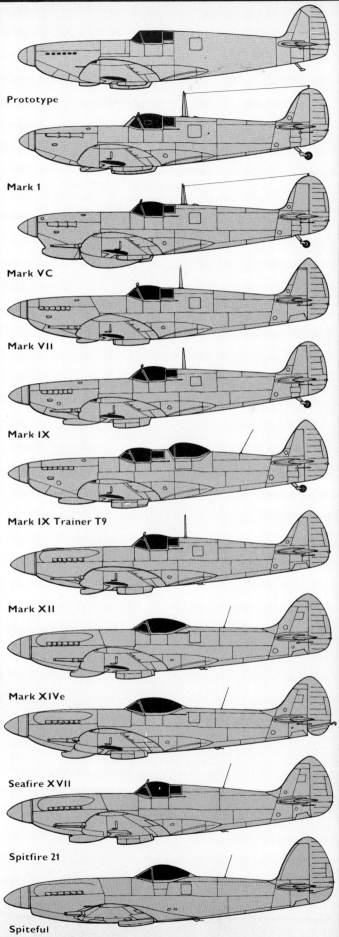

Prototype

Mark 1

Mark VC

Mark VII

Mark IX

Mark IX Trainer T9

Mark XII

Mark XIVe

Seafire XVII

Spitfire 21

Spiteful

APPENDICES

1. Performance Data

As the only Allied fighter to be continuously produced throughout the entire war period 1939–45, the development of the original Spitfire design to its ultimate version was truly remarkable in aviation annals. During those few years the Spitfire increased its engine power by 100 percent, its top speed by some 40 percent, its rate of climb by 80 percent, and its loaded weight by 40 percent.

The following table is intended to indicate some of the progressive improvements attained throughout the Spitfire's life span, but should not be regarded as a finite statement of actual performance figures capable of being reached by any specific Mark or variant. As explained in the main text, individual aircraft often exceeded – or fell short of – these recorded official pronouncements.

Mark	Maximum speed	Climb	Service Ceiling	Maximum range (miles)
I	355mph at 19,000ft	6.2 mins to 15,000ft	34,000ft	395
V	374mph at 13,000ft	7.5 mins to 20,000ft	37,000ft	1135
VII	408mph at 25,000ft	7.1 mins to 20,000ft	43,000ft	1180
VIII	408mph at 25,000ft	7 mins to 20,000ft	44,000ft	1180
IX	408mph at 25,000ft	6.7mins to 20,000ft	44,000ft	980
X	416mph at 27,000ft	5 mins to 20,000ft	44,000ft	1360
XI	422mph at 27,500ft	5 mins to 20,000ft	44,000ft	2000 approx
XII	393mph at 18,000ft	6.7 mins to 20,000ft	40,000ft	493
XIV	448mph at 26,000ft	7 mins to 20,000ft	44,500ft	850
XVIII	442mph at 25,000ft	7 mins to 20,000ft	41,000ft	850
XIX	446mph at 26,000ft	15.5 mins to 35,000ft	42,000ft	1550
F.21	454mph at 26,000ft	8 mins to 20,000ft	43,500ft	880
F.24	450mph at 19,000ft	5 mins to 20,000ft	43,000ft	965
Seafire I	365mph at 16,000ft	7.6 mins to 20,000ft	36,400ft	770
Seafire III	352mph at 12,250ft	8.1 mins to 20,000ft	34,000ft	725
Seafire 47	451mph at 20,000ft	4.8 mins to 20,000ft	43,000ft	1475

Some data relating to the first and last versions of the Spitfire 'family tree' gives a direct example of the extent of the aircraft's vast development in less than six years.

	Spitfire I	Seafire 47
Weight normal	5280lb	10,300lb
Weight overload	—	12,500lb
Wing area	242sq ft	244sq ft
Wing loading	24lb/sq ft	42.2lb/sq ft
Maximum horsepower	1050	2350
Power plant weight	2020lb	3650lb
Maximum speed	362mph	452mph
Maximum rate of climb	2500ft/min	4800ft/min
Time to 20,000ft	9.4mins	4.8mins
Weight of fire/second	4.0lb	12.0lb
Fuel capacity internal	85 gallons	154 gallons
Maximum range	575 miles	1475 miles
Rate of roll (400mph)	14 degrees/sec	68 degrees/sec
Factored wing loading	240lb/sq ft	464lb/sq ft
Maximum diving speed	450mph	500mph
Structure weight (percent)	33	31
Energy absorption of undercarriage	8300ft/lb	26,600ft/lb
Undercarriage stroke	4.9in	9in

The constantly improving performance range of each succeeding Spitfire Mark resulted from consistent attempts to refine relatively minor details of the airframe by the Supermarine design team. Some examples of the benefits accruing from such meticulous regard for detail are given below:

Refinement carried out	Speed increase in mph
Retractable tail wheel	5
Propeller root fairings	4
Chassis door panel	3
Whip aerial	0.5
Plain ailerons	6
Curved front windshield	6
Multi-ejector exhausts	4
Improved & waxed polished finish	9
Clipped wing-tips	1
Rear-view hood & deletion of mirror	1

With all these refinements it was possible to add almost 40mph to the stated maximum speed figure.

Below: **PRXIX PS853 in photo-reconnaissance blue livery.**

2. Squadron Use

Mark	Units
I &/or II	Nos 19, 41, 54, 64, 65, 66, 72, 74, 91, 92, 111, 118, 122, 123, 124, 129, 130, 131, 132, 137, 145, 152, 222, 234, 238, 249, 257, 258, 266, 303, 308, 310, 312, 313, 315, 331, 332, 340, 349, 350, 401, 403, 411, 412, 416, 417, 452, 457, 485, 501, 504, 602, 603, 609, 610, 611, 616 Also certain Air-Sea Rescue units
IV	Nos 140, 541, 542, 544, 680, 681, 683
V	Nos 19, 32, 33, 41, 43, 54, 64, 65, 66, 71, 72, 73, 74, 80, 81, 87, 91, 92, 93, 94, 111, 118, 121, 122, 123, 124, 126, 127, 128, 129, 130, 131, 132, 133, 134, 136, 145, 152, 154, 164, 165, 167, 185, 213, 222, 229, 232, 234, 237, 238, 242, 243, 249, 253, 257, 266, 274, 303, 306, 308, 310, 312, 313, 315, 316, 317, 322, 326, 327, 328, 329, 331, 332, 335, 336, 340, 341, 345, 349, 350, 401, 402, 403, 411, 412, 416, 417, 421, 441, 442, 451, 453, 485, 501, 504, 601, 602, 603, 607, 609, 610, 611, 615, 616, 1435
VI	Nos 66, 118, 129, 234, 313, 504, 521, 602, 616
VII	Nos 32, 41, 92, 118, 124, 131, 133, 152, 154, 417, 485, 602, 616
VIII	Nos 17, 20, 28, 32, 54, 67, 73, 81, 87, 92, 131, 132, 136, 145, 152, 155, 185, 253, 256, 273, 326, 327, 328, 352, 417, 452, 457, 528, 529, 548, 549, 601, 607, 615
IX	Nos 1, 6, 19, 32, 33, 43, 56, 64, 65, 66, 72, 73, 74, 80, 81, 87, 91, 92, 93, 94, 111, 118, 122, 123, 124, 126, 127, 129, 130, 131, 132, 133, 134, 135, 145, 152, 154, 164, 165, 185, 208, 213, 222, 225, 229, 232, 234, 237, 238, 241, 242, 243, 249, 253, 256, 274, 302, 303, 306, 308, 310, 312, 313, 315, 316, 317, 318, 322, 326, 327, 328, 329, 331, 332, 336, 340, 341, 345, 349, 350, 401, 402, 403, 411, 412, 414, 416, 417, 421, 441, 442, 443, 451, 453, 457, 485, 501, 504, 521, 595, 601, 602, 609, 610, 611, 1435
X	Nos 541, 542
XI	Nos 2, 4, 16, 26, 69, 140, 400, 541, 542, 543, 544, 680, 681, 682, 683
XII	Nos 41, 91
XIV	Nos 2, 11, 17, 19, 20, 26, 28, 41, 91, 129, 130, 132, 136, 152, 155, 229, 268, 273, 322, 350, 401, 402, 411, 412, 414, 416, 430, 443, 451, 453, 600, 602, 603, 607, 610, 611, 612, 613, 615
XVI	Nos 5, 17, 19, 33, 63, 65, 66, 74, 126, 127, 129, 164, 165, 229, 234, 302, 308, 317, 322, 329, 331, 340, 341, 345, 349, 350, 401, 402, 403, 411, 412, 416, 421, 443, 451, 453, 485, 501, 595, 601, 602, 603, 604, 607, 609, 612, 614, 615. Also AAC sqns: 567, 577, 587, 595, 667, 691, 695
XVIII	Nos 11, 28, 32, 60, 208
XIX	Nos 2, 58, 60, 81, 541, 542, 681, 682
F.21	Nos 1, 41, 73, 91, 122, 600, 602, 603, 615
F.22	Nos 73, 502, 504, 600, 602, 603, 607, 608, 610, 611, 613, 614, 615
F.24	No 80
Seafire I/III	Nos 801, 805, 807, 808, 809, 816, 833, 834, 842, 879, 880, 884, 885, 886, 887, 889, 894, 895, 897, 899 Training sqns 715, 718, 719, 741, 748, 759, 760, 761. Fleet Requirement sqns 728, 775
Seafire XV	Nos 802, 803, 804, 805, 806; 773 FR Sqn
Seafire XVII	Nos 800, 802, 803, 805, 807, 883, 1831, 1832, 1833, plus 736, 738, 759 Training units
Seafire 45	Nos 771, 778
Seafire 47	Nos 800, 804, 1833; 759 Training Sqn

NB Squadron numbers listed include RAF, Auxiliary (later, Royal) Air Force, RCAF, RNZAF, RAAF; both during and post-war years. Many of the Fleet Air Arm units listed held only small numbers of Seafires, often only six machines.

3. Spitfire Squadrons – Dispositions

7 July 1940			**6 June 1944 ('D-Day')**		
19	Duxford		1	Predannack	
41	Catterick		4	Gatwick	
54	Rochford		16	Northolt	
64	Kenley		26	Lee-on-Solent	
65	Hornchurch		33	Lympne	
66	Coltishall		41	Bolt Head	
72	Acklington		56	Newchurch	
74	Hornchurch		63	Lee-on-Solent	
92	Pembrey		64	Deanland	
152	Acklington		66	Bognor	
222	Kirton-in-Lindsey		74	Lympne	
234	St Eval		80	Detling	
266	Digby		91	West Malling	
602 AAF	Drem		118	Sumburgh (A Flt);	
603 AAF	Dyce (A Flt) &			Skeabrae (B Flt)	
	Montrose (B Flt)		124	Bradwell Bay	
609 AAF	Warmwell		126	Culmhead	
610 AAF	Biggin Hill		127	Lympne	
611 AAF	Digby		130	Horne	
616 AAF	Leconfield		131	Culmhead	
			132	Ford	
			165	Predannack	
			222	Selsey	
			229	Detling	
			234	Deanland	
			274	Detling	
			302	Chailey	
			303	Horne	

308	Chailey		441	Ford
310	Appledram		442	Ford
312	Appledram		443	Ford
313	Appledram		453	Ford
317	Chailey		485	Selsey
322	Hartford Bridge		501 AAF	Friston
	(Blackbusche)		504 AAF	Digby (A Flt);
329	Merston			Coltishall (B Flt)
331	Bognor		519	Skitten
332	Bognor			(part-equipped)
340	Merston		541	Benson
341	Merston			(A Flt); St Eval (B Flt)
345	Shoreham		542	Benson
349	Selsey		602 AAF	Ford
350	Friston		610 AAF	Harrowbeer
400	Odiham		611 AAF	Deanland
401	Tangmere		616 AAF	Culmhead
402	Horne		808 FAA	Lee-on-Solent
403	Tangmere		885 FAA	Lee-on-Solent
411	Tangmere			(Seafires)
412	Tangmere		886 FAA	Lee-on-Solent
416	Tangmere			(Seafires)
421	Tangmere		897 FAA	Lee-on-Solent
			899 FAA	Peterhead (Seafires)

In addition numerous 'second-line' units were part-equipped with Spitfires on this date, including such Meteorological Flights as 1401 (Manston), 1402 (Aldergrove), et al.

Below: **A ground view of a Mark V, AR 501.**

Bibliography

Should the reader wish to consult more detailed accounts of Spitfires the following selected titles and sources are recommended.

Spitfire Notebook, Aeroplane Spotter, 1945–46
The Book of the Spitfire, RP Pubs No 3, Real Photos, 1942
The Spitfire in Production, Aircraft Production, April 1942
The Spitfire, AEROPLANE, 12 April 1940
A Real Thoroughbred, FLIGHT, 26 September 1940
Air Publications (HMSO):
    AP 1565B, *Spitfire IIa & IIb*
    AP 1565E, *Spitfire Va & Vb & Vc*
    AP 1565J, P, & L-PN, *Spitfire IX, XI & XVI*
    AP 1565T & W-PN, *Spitfire XIV & XIX*
    AP 2280A, B, & C, *Seafire Ib, IIc & III* reprinted by Arms &
      Armour Press
Jane's All the World's Aircraft, 1938–55, L Bridgman; Sampson & Low

Spitfire, J W R Taylor; Harborough, 1946
Famous fighters of the Second World War, W Green, Macdonalds, 1957
British Naval Aircraft 1912–58, O Thetford, Putnam, 1959
Aircraft of the RAF since 1918, O Thetford, Putnam, 1978
Spitfire, B Robertson; Harleyford, 1960
RAF fighters of WW2, Vol 1, F K Mason, Hylton Lacey, 1969
Fighter squadrons of the RAF, J D R Rawlings, Macdonalds, 1969
Spitfire Special, T Hooton, Ian Allan, 1972
Aircam No 4, Spitfire Mk I–XVI, T Hooton, Osprey Pubs
Aircam No 8, Spitfire Mk XII–24, T Hooton, Osprey Pubs
Profile Publication No 41, *Spitfire I & II*
Profile Publication No 166, *Spitfire V*
Profile Publication No 206, *Spitfire Mk IX*
Profile Publication No 221, *Seafires*
Profile Publication No 246, *Spitfire Mks XIV & XVIII*
Camouflage & Markings No 1, Ducimus Books
Photo Reconnaissance, A J Brookes, Ian Allan, 1975
Spitfire at War, A W Price, Ian Allan, 1974
Spitfire – A Documentary History, A W Price, Macdonald Janes, 1977

Acknowledgments

The author would like to thank the individuals and agencies listed below for the use of their photographs and artwork.

Aircraft Productions: p 58 (bottom).
Air Portraits: pp 6–7, 52–53 (bottom), 54–55 (middle).
Anglia Aeropics: pp 6, 56 (bottom left).
Australian War Memorial: p 26 (top right).
Author's Collection: pp 8 (top left), 20 (top right), 23 (top), 24 (middle right), 26 (bottom left), 28 (top right), 29, 34–35 (bottom), 34 (top left), 35 (top left and top right), 37 (top), 38 (middle left), 40 (top right and bottom), 45 (top), 48 (top), 49 (top and

bottom), 50 (top), 52 (middle left), 53 (top left), 55 (top right).
Charles Brown: pp 14–15, 22–23.
Crown copyright: p 42 (middle left and top right), 48 (middle).
Director Publicity, Wellington, New Zealand; pp 27 (top), 28 (bottom).
Flight: pp 11 (bottom), 16 (top), 34 (top right), 45 (middle left), 46–47.
via NRL Franks: pp 30 (top left), 41 (top left).
FG Freeman Jr via T Hooton: pp 37 (bottom), 41 (top right).
Group Captain CF Gray: p 24 (middle left).
J Guthrie via T Hooton: p 36 (top left).
via T Hooton: pp 40 (top left), 45 (bottom right), 50 (middle and left), 51 (bottom).
via T Hooton/RCB Ashworth: pp 33 (bottom right), 52 (top left).

Robert Hunt Library: p 64.
Imperial War Museum: pp 13 (top), 15 (top), 18–19, 20 (top left and middle right), 20–21 (bottom), 23 (middle), 24 (top), 24–25 (bottom), 27 (bottom), 28 (top left), 30 (bottom), 31 (top), 33 (top left and top right), 36 (top right), 38 (top), 42 (top left), 44–45 (bottom), 54 (bottom left).
Mod (Air): pp 8 (top right), 16–17, 55 (top left).
K Munson: p 56 (middle left).
Photographic News Agency: pp 25 (top), 26 (bottom and top right), 42 (bottom left).
Public Archives of Canada: pp 53 (middle right), 54 (top left).
D Reid via T Hooton: p 36 (bottom).
via B Robertson: p 33 (middle right).
SAAF Museum: pp 32, 45 (middle left).

Taylor Picture Library: pp 38–39 (bottom), 42–43 (bottom).
via GJ Thomas: pp 38 (middle right), 41 (bottom).
US Air Force: pp 42 (middle right), 53 (top right).
Vickers-Armstrong (Supermarine)/CE Brown: pp 8–9 (bottom), 10, 11 (top and middle), 12–13 (bottom), 23 (bottom), 58–59 (top).
Gordon Williams: pp 44 (top), 55 (bottom right), 60–61, 62–63.

Artwork

Mike Badrocke: Cutaway on pp 56–57, line drawings on p 59.
Mike Bailey: Cover sideview.
Mike Trim: Sideview on p 57.

Below: Spitfires in formation line abreast cruising at 300mph between cloud layers at 6000ft.